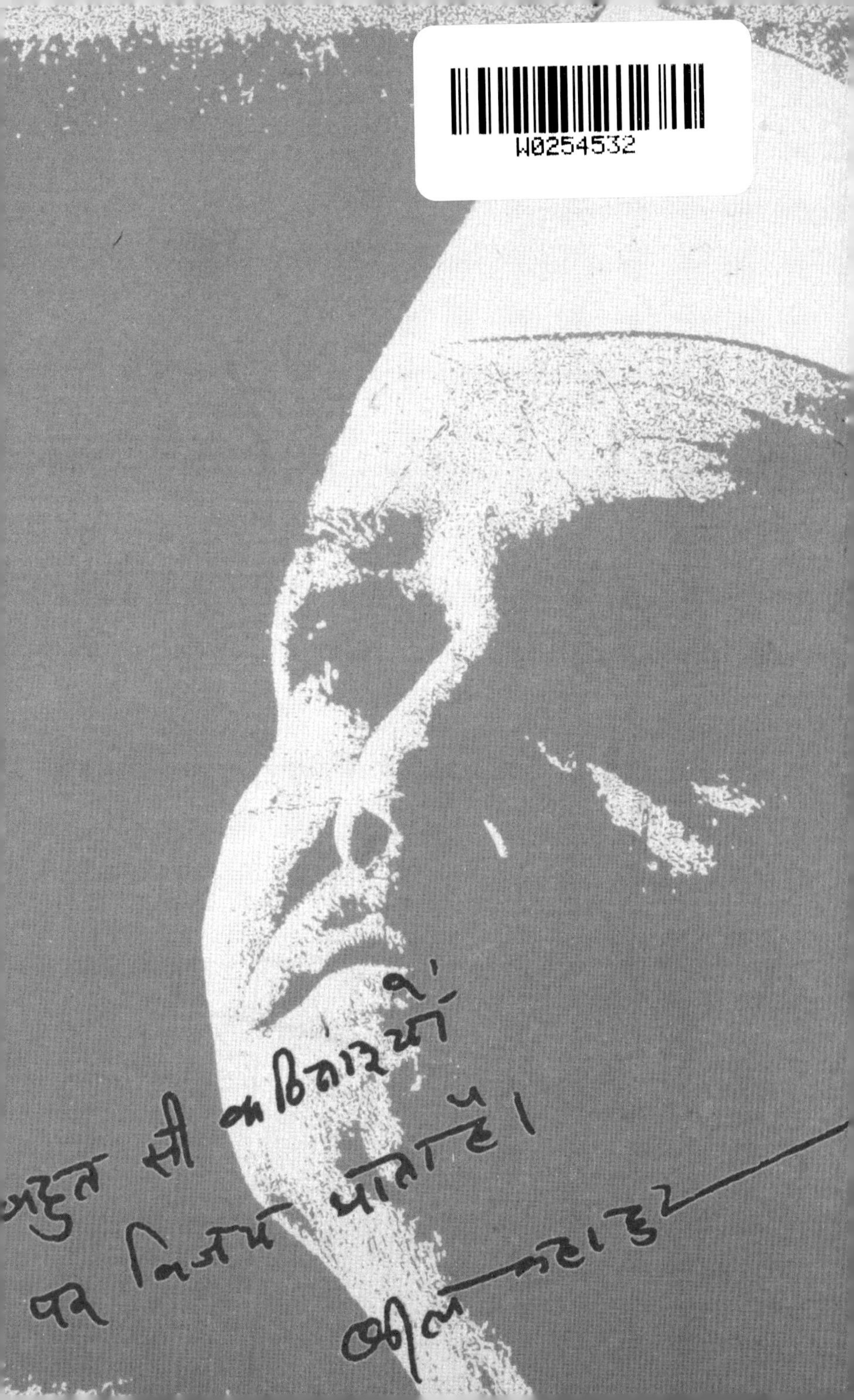
बहुत सी कविताएँ
पर निर्भर पाता है।

जय जवान – जय किसान

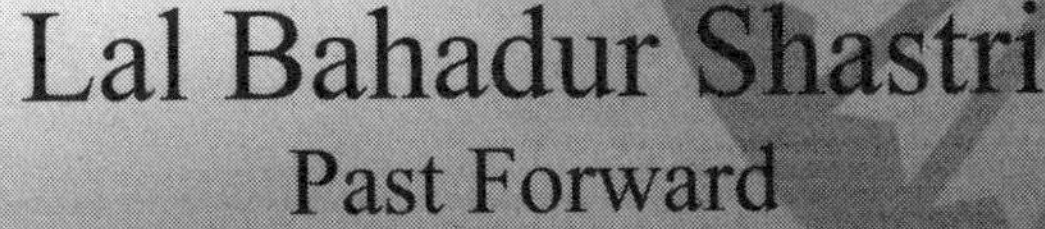

Lal Bahadur Shastri

Past Forward

Lal Bahadur Shastri

Past Forward

Sunil Shastri

KONARK PUBLISHERS PVT LTD
NEW DELHI · SEATTLE

KONARK PUBLISHERS PVT LTD
206, First Floor, Peacock Lane,
Shahpur Jat, New Delhi-110 049.
Phone: +91-11-41055065, 65254972
E-mail: india@konarkpublishers.com
Website: www.konarkpublishers.com

Konark Publishers International
1507 Western Avenue, #605,
Seattle, WA 98101
Phone: (415) 409-9988
e-mail: us@konarkpublishers.com

Second Impression 2018

Cataloging in Publication Data--DK
Courtesy: D.K. Agencies (P) Ltd. <docinfo@dkagencies.com>

Shastri, Sunil, 1950-
Lal Bahadur Shastri : past forward / Sunil Shastri.
p. cm.
ISBN 9788122007923

1. Shastri, Lal Bahadur, 1904-1966. 2. Prime ministers-India-Biography. 3. Shastri, Sunil, 1950- Family. 4. Fathers and sons. I. Title.

DDC 790.2095483 22

Designed and Layout by Idesign, New Delhi-110017
Printed at Thomson Press India Ltd.

Marshal of the Air Force Arjan Singh D.F.C.

Tele : 23014864

7-A, Kautilya Marg
New Delhi - 110021

Foreword

I got to know Lal Bahadur Shastri when he became the Prime Minister in 1964 but I learnt much about him just before and during the Indo-Pakistan war in 1965. He and the then Raksha Mantri, Y. B. Chavan, made an effective team to take political decisions. They often discussed the military capabilities with us to carry out the political decisions. I met him a few times in his house where only he and I discussed the Air Force broad plans in case ultimately our country had to go to war with Pakistan.

I found him to be very clear headed in his arguments and listened to me patiently without much interruption in a very friendly manner. He lived most simply and was often bare feet sitting near a small office table. He was really polite and came to his porch to see me off and at times apologized for keeping me late. During the 1965 war he met the Chief of Army Staff and myself every day. At times the discussion took place at Defence Committee of the Cabinet.

1965 war was the real test for his leadership in peace and war and, in my opinion, he passed with flying colours.

He laid down specific parameters within which the Armed Forces could operate. As far as the Air Force was concerned, he said that it should avoid attacking civilian population but hit any military targets. Thereafter, he did not interfere with any operations unless I wanted some clarifications.

Sunil Shastri narrates Lal Bahadur Shastriji's biography through anecdotes from his own life story, making this book a two-in-one kind; a biography within a biography. The story of Sunil's growth from a lad of sixteen to a mature politician is closely intertwined with the story of his father, who personified Gandhian values. In turn, the book offers glimpses of Shastriji's growth from his early years as a freedom fighter to his later years as Prime Minister. Shastriji's life story chronicles Indian history from the Indian Freedom Movement to Independent India's war with Pakistan in 1965 with its underlying focus on Gandhian values of honesty, simplicity and truth.

Sunil's book is a grateful tribute to his father with whom he spent the early impressionable years of his life. He was sixteen when he lost his Babuji but by that time he had inherited his father's legacy of selfless dedication to work for the upliftment of the poor and suffering majority of our country. Shastriji ever so gentle but firm made a request to his son – (which happened to be his last) – to visit the interior parts of India to understand the abject poverty experienced by the tribals and rural people. His ideas was to provide his son a true exposure of real India that lived not in cities and urban areas, but in villages and remote corners of the country. This visit opened Sunil's eyes to an unseen India and galvanized him to passionately devote his life to the cause of the poor. This book is the son's acknowledgement of his father's unique way of teaching him the values of selfless service and commitment to fellow humanity.

Sunil speaks of his father's guiding influence at all moments of crisis in his life. We are given vignettes of Shastriji's life revealing him as a people's leader and people's Prime Minister. Shastriji's exemplary humility and his extraordinary capacity to feel for fellow humanity had left an indelible mark on his son. Sunil affectionately recalls his Babuji in his various roles — as a gentle husband, a caring father, a compassionate leader, a strong and resilient Prime Minister and above all a practicing Gandhian who rose from humble beginnings to the highest office of the nation.

Written in a simple and direct language, shorn of frills and flourishes, Sunil conveys the father–son relationship that was kept alive by his mother. This is a must-read book, especially for the youth of the post-liberalization era, for its beauty and grace of a life, lived in elegant simplicity and austerity. Shastriji's life as stated in black and white is indeed a rediscovery of India and its values by that great man, Lal Bahadur Shastri.

Arjan Singh

28 October, 2010

Marshal of the Air Force

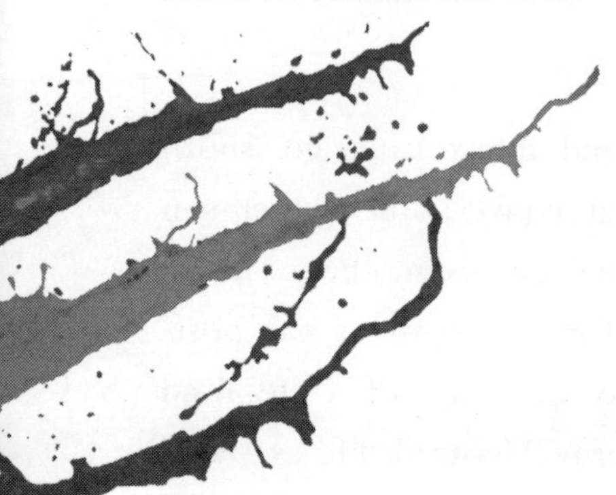

I am Sunil Shastri, my father's son, my mother's son and my leader Indiraji's disciple. I inherited from them the basic qualities needed to ward off challenges that one has to face in life and politics. My parents gifted me honesty and integrity while Indiraji instilled in me determination and self-belief to take on responsibilities. These qualities helped me reach out to the 'aam-admi'—the ordinary public—'the Common Man' so well popularized by the famous cartoonist R.K. Laxman. I have been fortunate to enjoy public support and affection that have been my biggest strength. Our people have always been the cornerstone of our democracy. Their enthusiasm, commitment and devotion, their readiness to make sacrifices when needed have zealously protected our democracy and freedom. I am indebted to my countrymen, the people of India who have given me a great tradition and a hoary, rich civilization. The more I realize my indebtedness to them, the more I despaire of my inability to cope with the huge responsibility of living up to the faith they have reposed in me as an active 'politician-son' of an illustrious father.

Often I feel disappointed and depressed that the political environment is not healthy and sound for me to discharge my responsibility. But I continue to have my dream for a New India and I wish to cross the stream. The only means to do so is to turn to my guardian angels for inspiration to my parents, my leader and my people to help me cope with the struggles true of any aspiring, well meaning and conscientious politician.

I entered politics, being the son of my father. I had a clean conscience, strength of character and a passion to work for the welfare of my people. But even as a senior minister in the government, I didn't have the freedom to do things that would benefit the people of this vast country. I encountered many problems—most of them beyond my control that stood in my way of translating

▲ Guru - Shishya (Sunil with Indiraji)

my ideas and schemes into action for the good of the people. It is in those moments of crisis between vision and action, between ideas and reality, between desire and fulfillment, between conception and creation, between desire and potency that I turned to the advice of my elders and seniors. I cherish even today the moments I spent with Indiraji that helped me to overcome my diffidence and rise up to the challenges. I had seen Mrs. Gandhi taking massive responsibilities on herself during the Emergency with great courage, strength and honesty of purpose. She knew that it would be difficult to dismount for anyone who rides a lion. Yet she showed indomitable strength and courage to take on lion's responsibility during Emergency and then with equal degree of courage and rectitude lift the Emergency even at a greater risk to her personal status and position. Her example gave me a lot of confidence and self-belief.

Let me return to my story at a momentous time in my life. After a long stint in politics in 1987, I felt deeply the hiatus between my values and contemporary outlook in politics. These were the times when in the name of Groupthink political parties insisted on uniform compliance to policies founded on pseudo ideologies. (Even today, Indian politics suffers from such a deep malaise) Those who resisted them and sought new directions based on values, ethics and principles were gagged and suppressed. I was one of those victims whose internal fire and passion for the right causes met with derision and hostility. I felt

▲ Mother of Mercy (Ammaji)

suffocated and choked and almost driven to seek political retirement. I sent my resignation to the Chief Minister who was at that point of time the protagonist (or shall I say, the antagonist) of my real life drama. In the later part of this book I will explain all that had happened that drove me to take this momentous step.

My next worry was how to convey my decision to my mother. There was also the added pressure of revealing to my brother my core feelings that had been formed and shaped by my father's integrity and truthfulness. I had been raised in a political environment, which inter alia made me understand and accept the fact that many things are not in our control. Hence the decision to chalk out one's own path was grounded on one's conscience and family upbringing and environment. One such incident merits mention here.

When I was in Lucknow, I saw a man in my house talking to my mother. I had seen him many times before—on the street outside my house whenever I strolled in and out of my house. He was an old, fragile man who was a milk vendor, cycling his way to sell milk to his customers. I used to wonder how this old man bent double with age continued with this arduous task of riding a cycle in all seasons—summer or winter to earn his livelihood. There was something about him that made me feel a sense of bonding with him, though I could not figure out the cause behind this sense of closeness to him. As I stepped out of my house to go to my place of work, I saw this old man talking to my mother who was recuperating from eye surgery. He had brought butter and ghee for her saying that they would help her recover and regain strength. "I wanted to give my best wishes to you and that is why I am here", he said. I was overwhelmed by his unconditional affection and care for my mother though I was intrigued as to who this person could be and how he had such a powerful hold over my feelings and emotions.

I assumed that he was close on to seventy years. Looking at him, I recalled what I had read about Mr. J.R.D.

Tata, who at eighty-three years of age had the same passion and dedication that he had in his early years to continue to work with the same zeal and dedication. The old milkman told my mother that he had to continue with his work as his son, influenced by modern times had moved out of the house and was living separately with his family. He had named him after me, Sunil, as he was born at the same time I was born. But unfortunately, Sunil, my namesake's commitment was much to be desired. He had given up all his family responsibilities in particular, towards his sister's marriage. Mother asked me to take responsibility to get the milkman's girl married. I agreed to bear all the expenditure and asked my wife Meera to finance the wedding expenses even if I had to be out of Lucknow. I did not want to be present at the wedding lest the old man should feel embarrassed at seeing me, the financier of his daughter's marriage. This incident gave me lessons in humility and self-abnegation that is often evidenced in many of our unremembered acts of kindness and pleasure. Life is founded upon such unusual relationships and these are the unusual instances that make us worthy of our human race.

My father's birthday, the 2nd of October is often co-terminus with Dussehra festival that is celebrated in different ways in different parts of India. It is the grand culmination of the 10-day annual Navaratri ('nine nights') festival marking the triumph of good over evil. For the Bengalis, this day marks the end of Durga Pooja celebrations, the preceding nine days being collectively referred to as 'Navratri'. It is dedicated to Mother Goddess Shakti, who incarnated in the form of Goddess Durga, to kill the mighty demon known as Mahishasura and free the world from his terror. For the others –both in the North and the South of India, it marks the victory of Lord Ram over the demon king Ravan. Somehow in my mind my gentle father personified the combined energy of Ram and Durga to preserve the territorial integrity of India from forces outside the country. Thus the observance and celebration of Babuji's birthday every year reinforced his magical presence around me, guiding me and directing me towards right action and decision in the larger interest of the nation.

October 2, 1986 was one special occasion when I was in Delhi to celebrate my father's birthday with my family members. It was Dussehra festival time with Vijaydasami just a week away. Many guests came to meet Amma and everyone had their own memory of my father. Mr. C.P. Srivastava who was Private secretary during Babuji's tenure as Prime Minister, was also present and he told us many anecdotes about Babuji that were unknown to us. Babuji's presence was all-pervading as though he was alive and in our midst. At one point of time, I almost felt that he was standing before us and seeking suggestions from Srivastavaji saying: "Srivastava Sahab, (note the courtesy he extended to his officers), I want a few suggestions from you."

While each one of us was lost in our individual world of our yesteryears with Babuji, my younger son came in. On my direction he greeted uncle Srivastava. Srivastavaji in reply asked him, "Son, what is your name?" Meantime my other two sons also joined us and I introduced all three of them—Vaibhav, Vinamra and Vibhor. Everyone appreciated the choice of these names though I had never disclosed to them the rationale behind their selection and their appropriateness and significance. Somehow on that day, I felt impelled to talk about this subject especially in the presence of my mother. I had identified each one of the names with one characteristic trait of Babuji. My sons were born long after Babuji's demise and therefore did not have the good fortune to know their grandfather.

I wanted them to carry forward his legacy of humility, greatness and bestowal of happiness all around him.

My eldest son, I named Vinamra meaning humility, that was so characteristic of Babuji who always remained egoless and free of pride. I called my second son, Vaibhav, keeping in mind Babuji's glorious personality. The last son, I gave the name Vibhor, symbolic of Babuji's genial quality that spread happiness around him. In my own way, I had through this selection of names honoured my father and showed my sons a glimpse of the path they should traverse to preserve the legacy of their grandfather. Both my elder brother and my mother were happy that I had thought so deeply in naming my sons. Amma took the three boys in her arms and her smile reflected her pride in her husband and her hope that her grand children will preserve and sustain his legacy. To all those cynics who derisively ask "What is in a name?", these names exemplify our great Indian tradition of naming children with the names of divinities or their divine characteristics. For me, Babuji has always been a divine soul and in my humble way I paid obeisance to him by naming my sons after his divine qualities.

When my sons grew up and requested me to take them to Red Fort on August 15 to watch the Prime Minister at close quarters, I was reminded of my early days when I had also persuaded my father to take me with him to Red Fort for the Independence Day functions so that I could see Prime Minister Pandit Nehru hoisting the flag from the ramparts of the Red Fort and listen to his Independence

▲ Swagatam (Shastriji greets foreign dignitaries)

day address. However, today children are kept in a separate enclosure away from the parents during such functions as a security measure. But in those days, there was no threat to security and meeting and moving close to the Prime Minister was never a daunting affair. Today seated with my wife and far away from my sons, I reminisced about the day when I had gone with Babuji to Red Fort for the Independence Day function. I could recall every detail about Nehruji—his movements and gestures, his great oratorical skills, the flourish with which he began and ended his speech and above all my impish and childish desire to hold his hand and move along with him. But every time I went near Panditji, he smilingly patted me on my back and sent me away. But I did not want to lose the opportunity to walk with him. Seeing me constantly trying to be close to Nehruji, the then Defence Minister Mr. Krishna Menon got annoyed and tweaked my nose causing me great pain. When Nehruji saw me in pain, he diplomatically told Mr. Menon: "Do you want this boy's nose to be as long as yours?" Mr. Menon at once released me. I moved towards Panditji who hugged me and held my hand till Babuji came and took me over. For me it was a dream come true.

While I was narrating this incident to my wife, Meera, it struck me that political life of a committed individual always interfered with his family life. This is nowhere better illustrated than in the distance that it brings in father–son relationship. Although Babuji never made me feel neglected in the midst of his awesome political schedule, I was often troubled in my early days by the emerging distance that was inevitable in our relationship.

Let me give an example of this disturbing aspect of being the son of Babuji when he was the Prime Minister of India. It was December 1965 when Babuji made an official visit to Rangoon, the capital of Burma (now called Myanmar). My younger brother Ashok and I were also part of his entourage. This was our first foreign visit, made more exciting as we were going with our Babuji and Amma. I was also tense and nervous as I was not going as my parents' son but as little ambassadors of India. With anxiety I asked Babuji as to what we were supposed to do in Myanmar. Babuji in his customary unflappable way told me not to worry and that I will be briefed about it in due course. He added that there may be meetings with peer group of students and I should be able to speak to them about our Indian culture and its diversities. I was petrified as to what I had to say about India. Babuji had his own quiet and calming influence on all those agitated like me. He said that India's diversity is so vast that hardly any one person will know everything about the country. As a young person, he said, I should focus on our unique secular culture that accommodates different religions and different communities and how modern independent India

has been shaped by our great leaders like Mahatma Gandhi and Pandit Nehru who had nursed this tradition.

We were taught to observe the code of conduct laid down for official visits—which meant that we were to behave with decorum as a part of the Prime Minister's group and not as that of his family. It was not a family outing but a state visit. We reached Rangoon and were taken to the State guest house. We brothers were told to occupy individual rooms—and not share the same room. This was a shock for us to be asked to stay separately. This first visit was disturbing, but was a new experience. We complained to Babuji that we were given separate rooms to stay. Babuji who was particular about following the code of conduct advised us to do what we were told till late at night, after which we could get together and stay in one room. Babuji was known for his punctiliousness but there was always a human side to his gentle commands. He understood our anxiety to stay alone and consented to step aside of the code of conduct only when it least mattered.

I realized for the first time my huge ignorance about my country. I wanted to learn more about the country, its cities and towns. On returning to India, I asked Babuji if I can travel with some of my friends on a tour of Bombay (now Mumbai). I was in for a rude shock when Babuji said: "Listen Sunil, you have just returned from a foreign tour. I want you to visit the rural belt of the country.

◀ Shastriji at his ancestral house in Ram Nagar (Past Revisited)

> "Try to understand those people who you have to serve. Try to know their problems and difficulties and get to know how they live."

As a young teenager I was disturbed, but there was no question of arguing with him. I expressed my disappointment with anger and resentment arguing that "If I don't go to Bombay, my entire plan would go waste but you are going to Tashkent."

Babuji noted the sarcasm in my tone but without getting irritated (an admirable quality with him) he said that he will arrange my visit to Bombay after his return from Tashkent, but for the time being, I will have to visit the rural areas of Madhya Pradesh and learn about the life there. It was impossible for me to refuse this gentle order and asked him what he expected me to do on this tour. He said that I should collect money for the National Defence Fund – even as small a sum as ₹ 10,000. What was of greater importance was my efforts to awaken the patriotism and passion in the people for their motherland—something that comes to the fore only during times of war but remains dormant during peaceful times. With enthusiasm I told him that my target would be ₹ 30,000 and when he heard me, he gave a warm appreciative smile something I can mentally visualize even today. But never did it cross my mind that, what was the last time he would smile at me and that was the last time I would see him.

I toured Madhya Pradesh rural belt, moving from one place to another, from one meeting to another. Babuji's quiet advice, his gentle and persuasive exhortations made me realize that India lives in her villages and understanding their poverty, their desires and their hard life was essential for anyone who desires to serve the country. This was my first lesson from Babuji. His insistence that I visited these areas was the first of the building blocks he had laid for my future development. He showed me the importance of taking the path less traversed to rural areas rather than the path well travelled to the glitter and glamour of cities like Bombay.

The tour to the rural belt was indeed exciting. Even today I can visualize the tour saved in my mental camera. The enthusiasm of the people was almost infectious and I soon began to feel a part of their history. I got so engrossed in listening to their life story, their sorrows, their expectations, their hopes and their fears that an emotional bond between me and the rural people began to build up. I realized the urgent need to convert their sorrows into happiness and to shoulder this responsibility in the days to come. Babuji had in his unique way redefined my future life as one of service to the poorest of the poor in our country.

I was just in my early teens and my father had given me the opportunity to see India at close quarters, not the glitter and glamour one sees in the cities but, the rural India with its teeming millions and their indomitable spirit to survive against poverty, hunger and destitution. I wanted to speak to Babuji and express my feelings, my dreams for those poor and my desire to serve them to my full capacity. I was grateful to Babuji who had opened my eyes to the real India and infused in me the passion and the urge to lift them up from the morass of despair. I was desperate to meet Babuji and share my excitement with him. I was almost like a man possessed and needed the calming and protective influence of Babuji to channel my emotions in the right and proper direction.

Within a span of two to three days, I was able to collect more than ₹ 15,000. Babuji had given me the target of just ₹ 10,000. Women came forward to give their jewellery to add to the government's collection for the welfare of the Indian soldiers.

It was the night of the 10th of January. Our itinerary had marked Ganj Basoda , a village in Vidisha. People had gathered in large numbers expecting me to arrive. While the meeting had been scheduled for early evening at 7.30, we were delayed by four hours as the previous meetings had extended beyond the allotted time. It was well past 11pm, but despite the cold night, the crowd had stayed on to welcome the son of their leader who had not only won the recently concluded war against Pakistan, but who had won a place in their hearts. I accepted all their wishes on behalf of Babuji and assured them that I would convey their feelings of love and gratitude to Babuji when I returned to Delhi. Just before the meeting concluded, I was informed that ₹ 2.5 lakhs had been collected for the Defence Fund. It was a very special moment for me. I was moved beyond words.

What a difference it was between Babuji's target of ₹ 10,000 and my own promise of ₹ 30,000 and the present collection that exceeded ₹ 3 Lakhs, a proof of the love and generosity of the poor people who lived in the rural areas of central India. I just wanted to fly and stand before Babuji and pour out all the emotions and happiness in my heart. I was just sixteen and raw in emotions when I started on my tour of the rural areas of Madhya Pradesh. Before the tour was over, I had grown-up, mature and experienced to understand life in its myriad colours, in its dark and gloomy side of suffering, its bright and golden side of love and warmth. I felt no longer a teenager but an adult with right emotions and right understanding. I felt a closeness to Babuji as I went to bed.

It was a little after 4 in the early hours when I was woken up and informed that all further programmes had been cancelled and I was to leave for Bhopal immediately.

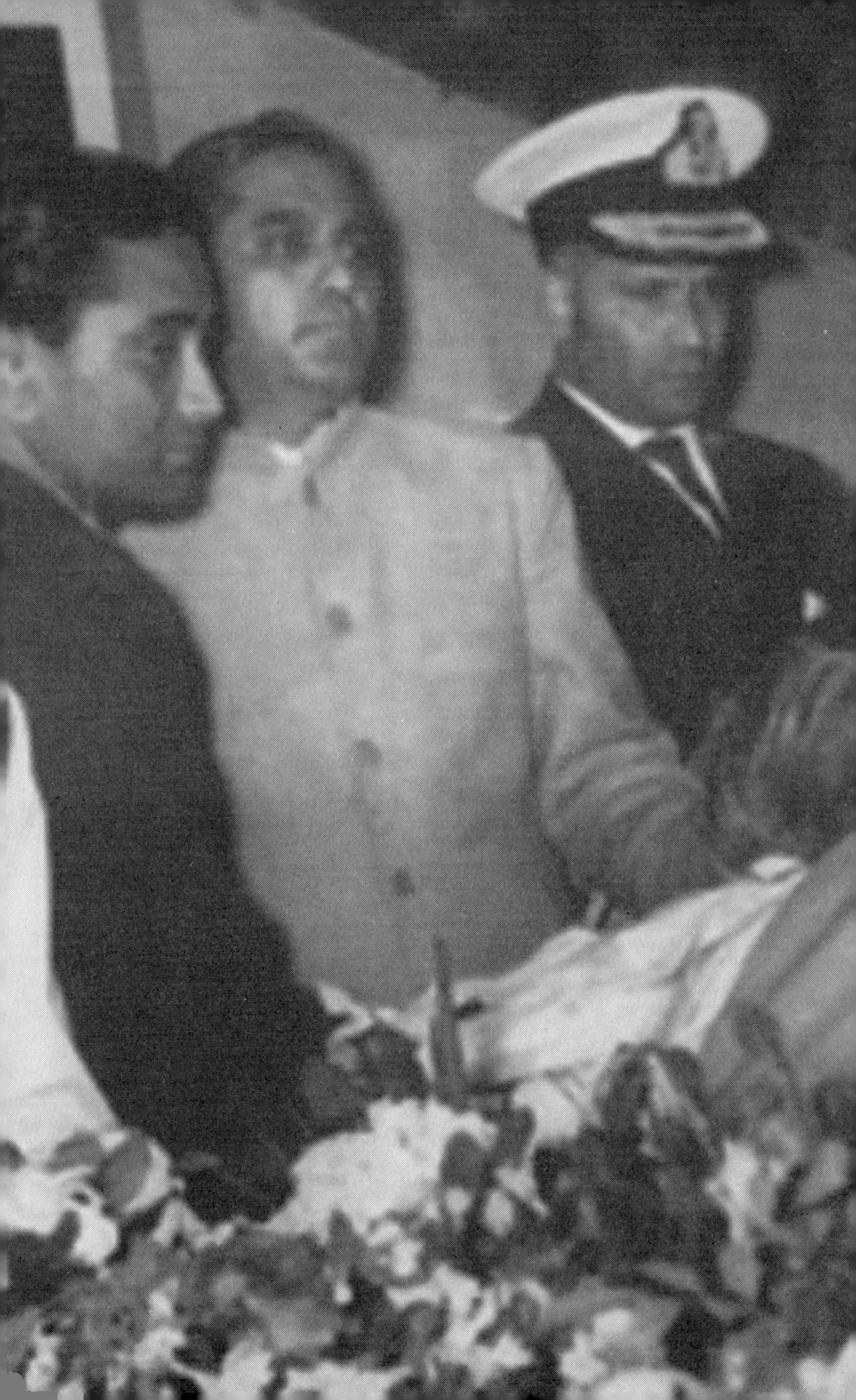

Light is gone: Babuji is no more

At that time Mr. Shankar Dayal Sharma who became the President of India two decades later was the leader of our party. I went to his room. I saw his eyes were moist, but neither he nor anyone in his room said anything to me. I felt strange as everyone was trying to avoid looking at me. It was Governer Shri K. C. Reddy's wife who told me in Raj Bhawan at Bhopal that I have to go to Delhi as my grandmother had expired.

From Bhopal we flew to Delhi. There were thousands of people at Palam airport. I felt a strange sense of misgiving. I thought that it was not my grandmother but my mother had deceased and that people were trying to spare me the sad news. Never did it flash in my mind that it could be Babuji. Rather simplistically I thought that since they all respected and loved Babuji, they had come to the airport to condole with him on my mother's death.

By car we sped home. As I reached home, I found everyone in tears. Hari Bhaiya, Anil, Ashok—all my brothers were weeping. No one spoke. I was almost numb with shock and kept standing at the entrance. Someone said, "Let us go to Amma". I thought I was being taken to see Amma's body. I was fighting my tears and tried to look courageous. As I took the first step on the stairs, I was stunned to see Amma coming out of her room in tears. I saw Amma without her bindiya, the symbol of Indian

married women. I couldn't move, couldn't take a step forward; I was numbed. Amma took me in her arms and that was the moment I realized I had lost my father.

I could never forget Amma's teary eyes of that day. I was devastated. All my expectations and hopes of reaching out to Babuji were shattered. All those aspirations and hopes I had woven in Madhya Pradesh had come unstuck. The garland of my dreams lay asunder as though someone had pulled the string that had bound the flowers. I could never ever share all those events and incidents that I had witnessed in Madhya Pradesh with my father. I felt miserable and helpless as there was no one except Babuji I had wanted to speak to and he had gone to eternal sleep.

At the most intense moment of pain, God gives us courage. I hugged Amma and with courage tried to look at her eyes flowing with tears. I made an unsuccessful attempt to wipe her tears and share her pain. I could never forget the sorrow and pain in her eyes.

It was then that I determined not to allow my personal grief to overwhelm my commitment to the cause of many a million grieving people I had met in those rural areas of Madhya Pradesh. At that moment I made a promise to myself that I will follow the path that Babuji had asked me to traverse and to this day my commitment stands. Throughout my life I decided that I would follow Babuji's parting advice to serve the masses who were in abject poverty. With Babuji's ideals to inspire me, I resolved to commit my future for the cause of the people in particular those in the rural areas.

Whatever he had asked me to do in Bhopal, I had done though I could not share my success with him. But the deprivation and the loss of his actual presence from my side gave me a steely resolve to continue with the task of doing things that will give him eternal peace and happiness. I felt his presence around me, guiding me, inspiring me and directing me to do what he alone would have done. I looked up at the skies to say "all is not well with the world; the stars shine still".

It was in 1980, when I became the Deputy Minister in the Uttar Pradesh government. I wanted my respected Amma to accompany me to Raj Bhawan for the oath taking ceremony. After the ceremony I touched her feet and sought her blessings. In simple and elegant words she said: "Do whatever work that is assigned to you with honesty, devotion and dedication." Her words brought to my mind my Dadi's advice to my father after he was sworn

SARVODAYA

in as the Prime Minister of India. With a lot of affection she told him: " Nanhe, no matter whatever happens to you, you should see to it that nothing ever happens to our motherland. You should serve your country wholeheartedly without caring about yourself." Life had come a full circle to me at that moment. These women though not formally educated, were aware of life's lofty principles and ideals. They valued honour more than the personal safety and well-being of their sons. They seem to sum up Shakespeare's words about honour that said:

> From lowest place when virtuous things
> proceed,
> The place is dignified by the doer's deed:
> Where great additions swell and virtue none,
> It is a dropsied honour: good alone
> Is good without a name…
> The property by what it is should go,
> Not by the title

Three words made me realize that designations such as Minister, Deputy Minister, Prime Minister etc., gain credibility and stature not because of the titles, but solely by the addition of virtue and goodness of the doer's deeds. I could hear in my mother's exhortation the echo of my grandmother's advice to her son. I understood the importance of their words that reinforced what Babuji had told me prior to my visit to the rural areas of Madhya Pradesh.

> Look back and get experience
> Look forward and see hope
> Look around and see reality
> Look within and feel confident

I could at any given point of time recall the experience of warmth and affection the rural people of Madhya Pradesh had given me—the 16-year old son of Babuji who was their most worthy and revered leader. With that experience, looked forward with hope of succeeding in my sole mission to help all those in need of my assistance. The visit to Bhopal had also enabled me to look around and understand reality both in its memorable moments of joy and despair. Babuji's parting advice before he left on that fatal trip to Tashkent helped me feel his eternal presence and grow in confidence to do things as he would have done.

My mother frequently visited me at Lucknow during my ministerial tenure. During one of her visits, I told her that I had been eating meals made by my wife and for a change would like her (Amma) to cook my dinner. By then Amma had grown old but she was happy to cook as I had asked her. It was a wonderful meal indeed and my sons could not stop praising her. I took her hands and kissed

them and said: "If today someone were to ask me how precious these hands are, I would not know how many millions worth they are. It is impossible to gauge the price of mother's love."

When I looked at her expecting her face to be lit with joy, I found her eyes filled with tears. The contentment that was there after feeding me had disappeared. She was trying to wipe her tears. I felt a sudden pang of remorse that I had said something inadvertently. I went and sat next to her and insisted on knowing what was it that I had said to cause her such a pain. With great difficulty she replied that my remarks about the invaluable worth of her hands reminded her of Babuji's remark during the days of our struggle for independence. She had then cooked a nice meal for him after his return from prison. He complimented her for the excellent meal almost repeating what I had told her a few minutes earlier. Babuji had then told her, "If ever anyone asks the value of these hands, I would say millions and millions." My mother's eyes were moist with emotions as I hugged her. The tears were of joy and pride, almost affirming that her husband continued to live in her sons.

"If ever anyone asks the value of these hands, I would say millions and millions."

Babuji in his short tenure as the Prime Minister of India (1964–66) had shown to the world that India is a strongly united country that rises as one nation when provoked by hostile forces from outside. A tiny and frail looking person, he had shown to the world, the strong steely man within when he led the country to victory in the war against Pakistan. He was a follower of Gandhiji (whose birth date he shared) who found the real India in the villages and recognized that development of agriculture on par with military might was the key to India's prosperity. He coined the slogan

"Jai Jawan, Jai Kisan"

as his salute to the defenders and nourishers of Indian democracy. This slogan encapsulated Babuji's passion for a strong, vibrant resilient India; its impact on the masses was electrifying that had to be experienced to be believed. Alas! he did not live long to preserve, sustain and strengthen a rejuvenated India! Less than two decades after his death, in 1984, after the assassination of Mrs. Indira Gandhi, the nation was once again at the brink of disintegration.

Today in 2010, two and a half decades after 1984, we recognize the increasing difficulty of re-building a united India. The nation is continuously assaulted and buffeted both by terrorists and violent rioters from within. Like

जय जवान जय किसान

JAI JAWAN JAI KISAN

many of my patriotic countrymen, when I raise my hand in salute to the National Flag on ceremonial occasions such as the Republic Day and the Independence Day a deep sense of misgiving and sadness disturbs me at the thought of a potential disintegration of the country. In the '80s, soon after Mrs. Gandhi's death, the country had risen as one nation to the clarion call of Rajiv Gandhi to the youth of India: "Bharat Banao" (build India). I also responded to it with my song

> "Miljulkar sab aao/Bharat desh banao"
> (everybody come together, unite to build India).

But today, two decades after Rajivji's assassination (1991), I am painfully compelled to rewrite the song changing 'banao' to 'bachao' (from 'build' to 'save')

> "Miljulkar sab aao/Bharat desh bachao"
> (May everyone come together and save the Nation).

These lines seem more appropriate for this disturbed period. It is time we thought of ourselves as citizens of India and took up the responsibility of saving the nation from terrorism, violence and crime unleashed by all those who neither understand nor appreciate the gift of a vibrant, independent democratic nation gifted to us by our great Indian leaders.

No doubt, from the time of Independence in 1947 to this day, we have progressed in all fields. Even in these hard times of global economic recession, our economic growth rate has not stagnated. We are now a nation to be counted among the developing nations and sooner than later we will be inducted into the UN Security Council. Our stature has grown, thanks to our advancement in Science and Technology, Industrial and Agricultural development, Medical and Engineering growth, not to leave out Computer Software business. However, despite all this progress, we occupy a lowly 129th rank out of 145 nations in Human Development Index. We have not been able to raise human quality to higher levels and build future Citizens of India

◀ Sunil with the Nehru scions (Sunil, Rajiv and Indiraji)

and the world. The sense of unity and togetherness, the sense of love and harmony that has been a part of our pluralistic and secular state is missing. Our education has failed to produce free citizens who can call their minds their own; sadly we lag behind in learning to be human beings capable of love and reasoning. We have become narrow citizens who have difficulty in understanding all those who are different from us in terms of religion, class, caste and creed. The question how to build the nation once again on the principles of unity, integrity and humanity bothers me. Why are we not able to re-ignite love for our motherland in every Indian's heart? Of course it surfaces in times of crisis when there is trouble for the country. But to harness that love during times of peace is equally important so that we present a strong united front that no power in the world can ever challenge. We have to find a way to create the right physical and social environment so that our children can inculcate love, respect and devotion for their motherland. They have to be taught how to be an ideal citizen—one who feels a sense of loyalty to all his fellow citizens irrespective of what background they belong to. Mutual love and respect for all individuals despite religious, social and political barriers will help us think and act both as citizens of India and citizens of the world. The urgent task for all political parties and for all those engaged in social causes for the nation's development and progress is to promote the feeling of Indianness in the minds of the people. Their agenda should be to promote respect for our National flag, our Constitution, our National Anthem (which incidentally has been chosen by UNESCO as the Best National Anthem in the world) and this will translate into respect for National unity and integrity. India is a huge country where diverse customs, languages, religions, cultures and practices provide a panorama of its tradition and heritage. But threading through these different regions and their practices is the concept of Bharat that is India. The quintessential Indianness is not to be lost in the midst of this diversity. It is our duty to see that this generic quality of being an Indian is not subsumed by narrow regional partisanship but that it shines through all the differences that are a part of the whole nation. If we fail to arrest the inter-regional, inter-state and inter-religious conflicts, we may soon be dismembered. Like the legendary Humpty Dumpty, we will also have a great fall but will not be able to put together again as India or Bharat.

Let us not leave the nations' future to a small group of narrow minded bigots who believe in creating disturbance for their own personal gain and who turn the national diversity from being an asset into a liability. They exploit the raw and naïve emotions of the uninitiated youth and make them rise in revolt against all those who do not belong to their region. The water dispute between states is an example of how political parties whip up frenzy among people in the name of regional loyalty. By falsely orchestrating potential danger to their existence and livelihood from fellow citizens in the adjoining state, they arouse unhealthy passions that result in wanton destruction of life and property of many thousands.

I had inherited this legacy of love for the Nation, love for the Tricolour from my family. I know the strength of the bond that unites me with my nation. Babuji's address on our Independence day in 1965 is etched in my memory. Babuji said: "Whether we live or not, this country will live. This Tricolour will live. Today this country and this flag stand as a symbol of our unity as a nation, but what is missing from our midst is our national character and our love for our motherland."

Hence I have changed my song today:

"Miljulkar sab aao/Bharat desh bachao"
(May everyone come together and save the Nation).

"Whether we live or not, this country will live. This tricolour will live. Today this country and this flag stand as a symbol of our unity as a nation, but what is missing from our midst is our national character and our love for our motherland."

I salute the Tricolour while watching the Republic Day celebrations—the Tricolour in which I have immense faith and belief, the Tricolour that is our legacy, the Tricolour that represents courage and sacrifice, peace, truth, faith and chivalry.

Babuji once said: "Nanak nanhe he raho, jaise nanhi doob, aur rukh sukh jayega, doob khoob bhi khoob"(Remain a small one as small as grass other plants will wither away, but the grass will remian ever green)

I had a wintry experience when I remembered these words of Babuji. I was returning home with my wife, Meera after attending a marriage. The night was foggy and chilly causing poor visibility. We had rolled the windows up to mitigate the severity of the weather but the chill had got into our bones and we longed to reach home and sit before the heater and warm ourselves. We were close to the gate when Meera startled me with her question: "Did you see that?" I couldn't figure out what she was asking nor could I see anything before me in that night of dark visibility. Meera had peered through the darkness to see a hut at a short distance from my home. She explained that a woman had started living in that hut with her two children. I followed Meera's direction and saw a ramshackle of a hut that had for its roof just a piece of cloth and was open on all four sides. On a broken cot, the kids and the mother were sleeping on that chilly night, covering themselves with a single quilt. I could mentally visualize a contrasting scene where many others like me comfortably sleeping behind closed doors on mattresses with heaters on and with quality quilts to warm us. I felt like a sinner. Despite the heat radiating within the room, I felt frozen at the sight of the chilly hut where lay huddled the mother and her two kids. I couldn't get to sleep; Meera was also restless. We both were feeling guilty at the vast disparity between our luxury and their poverty. My mind struggled to come to terms with the reality that this is our motherland. I realized that there will be many thousands of mothers and kids like them, experiencing the hard chilly wintry weather. I told Meera: "Let us go and give our woollens and quilts to them." Meera as ever was one step ahead of me as she switched on the lights and collected the warm clothes and quilts and rushed out to the hut in the cold, dark night to provide them some comfort. I saw Meera leaving. I knew that providing timely relief was the best that could be done, but then, those three were lucky to be at our doorstep. I asked myself who is to care for the many suffering millions like them who needed such help and yet could not be reached!

I had no solution to offer. I lacked ideas to provide relief to the poor and the marginalized millions in the country. All that I experienced was great anguish at my impotence. I wished that Babuji was near me to guide me and lift me out of my winter of discontent.

But in the absence of Babuji, I often turned to Amma to solve many of my problems. She was schooled in Babuji's ideals and her experience with Babuji had given her the strength to face any problem.

She said that for Babuji there was no word as 'impossible'. For him the word meant 'I—am—Possible' to suggest that it is possible for me to do anything.

She helped me understand that if Babuji could face all hurdles with a calm composure, then I should prove worthy of being his son. Often I visited her in Delhi and particularly on festive occasions. I derived a great deal of strength and courage from her to discharge my duties as a public servant. During one of my visits coinciding with Dussehra festival, I was taking a stroll with my wife and recalling my memories of Babuji. My mother was staying in the same bungalow which Babuji had occupied when he was Prime Minister. Babuji used to spend most of his time in a small room adjacent to the verandah. (Now this room has been converted into a small museum in his memory). While walking through the verandah, I felt someone was watching the two of us. I went near the room but found no one and continued walking up and down the verandah.

Shastriji stepping out of a defence aircraft ▶

Again I felt the presence of someone looking at us. It was Amma. To my question as to why she was watching us, she avoided a direct answer, but as I insisted with the question, she said : "Watching you both together reminded me of my good old days. Just like both of you, your Babuji and I also used to walk whenever he got free time. Hence I remembered how busy he used to be."

Amma was nostalgic and in her characteristic way, remembered how her husband made time for her amidst his packed schedule. Babuji was not only the Prime Minister, but he was also a family man. He always had the interests of all those who needed him. I remember my refusing my mother's request to get someone a job. She said that Babuji would have never refused to help the needy and the deserving people who sought his help. I was stung to the quick and sullenly answered that times have changed since Babuji's days and things are not that simple as they were before. Amma 's answer almost sounded like Babuji when she pointed out that Babuji never allowed circumstances to dictate what he felt was the right thing to do. Without ever compromising any of his principles, he was able to take control of circumstances and act with patience, compassion and rectitude to help those who approached him for assistance.

I felt embarrassed as Amma gave the example of Babuji both as a strong Prime Minister as well as a gentle and human being who was at ease with both his political and social responsibilities. To be a master of all circumstances and to act without compromising one's principles is a difficult proposition. Amma in a quiet way had spoken to me about the complete man that Babuji was. I promised Amma that I will try to follow in his footsteps.

Soon I found that it was easy to promise to Amma that I will be another edition of Babuji, but difficult to keep up to it. I had made a conscientious choice of being in politics having seen Babuji both as a politician and a family man. But I did not understand the heavy demands on a politician's time. Being in the world of politics and surrounded by people, one tends to be far away from his people, family and domestic situations. Despite my sincere efforts, I couldn't give sufficient time to my family. Returning home after a day's hard grind, I always preferred to stay home and not step out to socialize with family and friends. On one such occasion when I came back home, Meera reminded me of my promise to meet a friend for dinner. I snapped at her saying I had no energy left at the end of the day to go partying. Meera insisted, as the friend had made several calls to enquire about our visit. Reluctantly, we left a little after 10 in the evening. In the absence of my driver who had gone home, I had to drive my personal car. Tired and angry, I observed that people's interest in me was purely selfish and their insistence on my visiting them was to seek personal favours. Meera, faulted me for ascribing selfishness and personal interest to my friend for inviting me to dinner with his family after I had given him the specific date and time. Meera counselled me: "He is your friend. You consider him your friend. Friendship is not based on selfishness". Meera's observation shook me to the core especially when I found the entire family including the children were waiting for us. I felt sorry for my outburst (luckily only Meera had heard it) and realized that I was the selfish person nurturing my fatigue without appreciating the warmth and affection of my friend and his family. When I returned home there was no trace of my earlier tension and fatigue. I learnt to value the importance of so many people who had showered their love on me, supported me in times of crisis and helped me in all my endeavours to honour the promise I had made to Babuji to serve the people of India. Without them I could not have done even a fraction of what Babuji had expected of me.

Babuji had implanted the sapling of public service in my heart. He did not live long to water it and see it grow. But it survived and stayed within me all these years.

I was 16 when Babuji died and at 30, I was old enough to enter public life to serve the nation. But I felt rudderless lacking guidance and direction. I thought of Indiraji who was for me more a mother than a leader. I approached her and asked her to give me a chance to actively participate in politics. I told her: "I wouldn't promise big things but I would definitely leave no stone unturned to continue this family relationship which Babuji had built with Pandit Nehru.I just want an opportunity to serve."

I well remember the look in her laughing eyes. She was gentle and caring and said: "If an opportunity comes, we will definitely consider your request." After many days, I met her at her residence—plush with green lawns. She had a way of infusing confidence and trust in one's own ability. I could feel a sense of reassurance of my ability to carry out the mission that Babuji had given me—to serve the masses. She said that I should stand for elections for the UP Vidhan Sabha from Gorakhpur constituency. Until then my knowledge of Gorakhpur was limited to a speck on the map of India.

It was election time. My mind was seething with worrisome questions about getting a positive mandate from people I had never associated with. A strange fear gripped me. I was assailed with doubts how at 30, I will be able to give up my family life, keep away from my wife and my children and plunge headlong into the political arena.

Active politics had always remained a distant dream till it had come close to becoming a reality. I almost wished it had remained a dream. If I failed in politics, then what next... It was this troublesome question that brought to my mind Babuji—his greatness, his selfless love for the country, his dimunitive personality that cloaked the strong steeliness in him. He had always placed his nation before his family. He had entered active politics very early in life and participated in the freedom struggle. For him, freedom of the nation had always assumed priority over family concern and he had courted prison life while fighting the British.

The confusion in my mind cleared when I remembered Babuji's sacrifices at the altar of his nation. I decided to fight the elections if I was offered a ticket and I was certain that with Babuji's blessings and Indiraji's love, I would get the ticket for Gorakhpur. No more was I racked with doubts and misgivings. The entry into politics meant giving up my bank job with no guarantee of success in the political field. There were many who advised me against joining politics as I was not of that age when I could afford to take risks. But I had made up my mind. At 30, I had this opportunity to serve the people as Babuji had done all his life. Such a time would never come if I let go of this opportunity. What shall be done tomorrow can as well be done today. or "time and tide wait for no man". If I have to fulfill my promise to Babuji, I should get started at the first opportunity.

I went and stood before Amma and spoke to her about my dilemma to join or not to join politics. My wife and children were also with me when I asked her. She asked me why I wanted to enter politics. This was a very significant question as it helped to clear my own mind. I said: "Amma, there are many things related to Babuji that inspire me. There were so many dreams, so many desires of Babuji which remain unfulfilled. He had given me the responsibility to complete them. I had stored these dreams in my heart and now is the time to translate them into reality. Hence my decision to take this first step into politics. Further Indiraji has also given me the confidence that I will win in Gorakhpur." Amma stared at me for a while and laughed saying "Then why are you asking me?" She shocked me by adding "Ask Babuji". Confused and surprised I asked her how can I ask him who is no longer with us. She asked me to go to his Samadhi and put two chits and pick one of them to get the answer. She said that whenever she was in a dilemma and needed his advice, she did this.

I went to his Samadhi but prior to picking up one of the chits, I was assailed by worrisome thought—if the answer was in the negative, how would I accept it? Would that not be an end to all my dreams, goals and aspiration! Can this one chit picked at random determine the course of my life? All my efforts to convince Indiraji and get my nomination will prove futile if on the basis of a negative verdict I give up my plan to stand for election. Countering these questions was my doubt about my own caliber to be a politician. I wondered whether I had even a tenth of Babuji's greatness to join politics.

I stood before his samadhi and paid homage to Babuji. I prayed to him to give me the right direction as I placed the two chits. With eyes closed I picked one of them and handed it to Amma. It was a 'yes' chit. I hugged her and she kissed and blessed me. Even at this moment I feel her presence, her warmth, her love and her care. Indiraji asked me if I was confident of winning. Indiraji had a perceptive eye to look into the future. I told her that I was confident of succeeding and would try my best to live up to her expectations. The die was cast. I left for Gorakhpur after taking Amma's blessings and filed my nomination papers. My political journey began from that moment—a journey that Babuji had taken years back, a son's journey in his father's footsteps.

The nomination papers had to be filled in by 3 pm. For many who had assembled there, I was Babuji's son. I reached just in time much to a mixed gathering of those who wished I had stayed away and those who saw in me the return of Babuji. I was not used to this mixed signal of acceptance and hostility to my candidature, but remembering Babuji's experience in handling any charged atmosphere, I was not unduly troubled. I had inherited this legacy from Babuji to accept friends and foes alike in one's political career.

I was in the process of filing my nomination when a group of 10–15 boys stormed into the room. One who seemed to be the leader mockingly observed: "This lad sent to contest is an outsider. Almost looks as though fallen from the sky!" I was startled to be referred to as an outsider, a stranger, a foreigner in my own homeland. I resolved to erase all such imagined differences and prove to my constituency that I was one of them, an Indian like

▼ The future is here

anyone of them. The best way to win over an enemy is to make friends with him.

I placed my nomination paper before him and requested him to sign as my proposer. Such a friendly gesture from me disarmed him and without a protest he signed for me. What started almost like a fisticuff became a handshake! This young man had been viewed as a whimsical bully consorting with wrong people and pursuing wrong and unethical means to force everyone into submission. In my own way I changed him very much in the manner of Babuji who had always succeeded in bringing people on to the right track.

Today the erstwhile bully is my close friend. I remember going with him to attend a school function in the city. As the chief guest I had to address the students. But I did not want to adopt a hectoring tone to give the young children moral advice. I was careful not to preach or speak a high falutin language that zipped past their understanding. I spoke to them more as a parent than as a political leader and this appealed to them and their parents. I told them about my school days when I was a student of St. Columbus in Delhi. Babuji was then the Home Minister. Those were the days when corporal punishment like caning was in use if students failed to submit their holiday homework on their return from vacation. I had spent the entire vacation playing cricket and my homework was nowhere near submission. I feigned stomach ache to escape going to school, but Amma wouldn't listen. So I went to Babuji, sat at his feet with my head on his lap. He asked me in his gentle fashion: "Aren't you ready for your school?" I enacted the drama of being sick. Babuji said "Ok" and returned to his office files. I kept on sitting at his feet till the tonga (horse cart) arrived and both my brothers got in. Babuji looked up from the files and quietly said: "The tonga has left, but in future you should not have this kind of a stomach ache." Without raising his voice and punishing me, Babuji had made me understand the folly of faking illness. He had a gentle way of teaching children and he never resorted to anger and punishment to make us understand what is right and wrong.

▲ Shastriji, a Champion with champions.

> "The tonga has left, but in future you should not have this kind of a stomach ache."

My young friend, seated next to me, remained quiet, lost in his world. After my narration, he came close to me and took my hand – a tender gesture that spoke of his intense gratitude to me for making a new person of him. My elder son Vinamra hugged me saying, "Papa, you spoke very well today." His words took me back by 15 years. As a fifteen year old at that time, I had listened to Babuji who was the then Prime Minister of India. When he returned home after the speech, everyone greeted him and complimented him on his inspiring speech. I was shy and waited for him to be alone with Amma when I told "Babuji, you spoke very well today."—the very same words my son had spoken to me that day. I could not say anything more as I was choked with mixed emotions of pride and joy, admiration and respect for my father. Babuji asked me "What did you like in my speech?" I had scribbled a few sentences in a paper and I read them to him saying that he could have concluded his speech on those lines. I spoke not to the Prime Minister of India, but as a son to his father. Babuji ever so humble accepted my suggestion and said "Next time whenever I speak on this topic, I will definitely add what you have said." My son had continued the lineage from grandfather to his son and then to his son's son by a repetition of words I had spoken years ago.

Amma was not too happy about what she felt was impertinence on my part to advise Babuji. But I learnt from her after many years how Babuji counseled her not to suppress the wishes and thoughts of the young lest their dreams and ideals get shattered.

I wanted to talk to Meera on bringing up young adolescents. But somehow I could not get the proper time to discuss this issue with her. I had an official engagement in Nainital and Meera and I decided to go a day earlier so that I could squeeze at least a day to be with my family. I was waiting for this holiday for long. I reached Lucknow to pick up Meera and children a day prior to leaving for Nainital. I found Meera busy with her daily chores. She had not packed. I learnt from her that only Vibhor (youngest son) had leave and the other two didn't have. She said that she could not leave them behind though I suggested the two of them could join the officers coming for the scheduled meeting the following day. Meera was not agreeable and, in anger I told my personal secretary to cancel the tickets for that day and that we would all travel together the next day. This, in effect meant my cancelling the one day holiday I wanted to spend with the family. I got up midway from the dining table and did not exchange a word with my wife that night. But the following morning I was calmer and realized that the fault was not entirely Meera's and we both had to share the responsibility for calling off a much desired holiday. I did not appreciate Meera's problem of getting the house whitewashed to receive Amma who was to come for Diwali which was few days away. And she did not realize how much I needed this holiday. Both of us were at fault. Every single incident for me was a repetition of an act played earlier by Amma and Babuji. They also had their little bickerings but Babuji never reacted in anger. He was wise and tolerant and kept quiet for Amma to let off her steam. This had a magical effect on her. She would cool down in no time and prepare Babuji's favourite dish to make up. Babuji without nursing any grievance would ask her with a smile: "Now, has your anger cooled down?" Deep down in my heart I appreciated the value of patching-up—a quality so essential for a politician who confronts people of different ideologies, temperament and attitude. I always wished Meera understood my difficulty in balancing private and public life. But that was almost asking for the moon. Hence I decided to follow Babuji and seek reconciliation with Meera after every petty quarrel.

Babuji's relationship with his mother seemed to belong to the epic eras of the Ramayana and the Mahabharata. Writing about it makes me nostalgic and yearn for those days when power and position bowed before parents and elders in the family. Babuji was the Prime Minister in charge of all national and international issues but once back home he was just his mother's son. My grandmother who used to stay in her meditation room would sense the arrival of Babuji from office and softly say "Son, have you returned?" Despite all his tension and preoccupation with matters of importance, Babuji would at once go to her room and sit with her at least for 5–10 minutes. Her love and care for her son, albeit for a very short time, would rejuvenate him and help him get over the day's fatigue and worries.

Today, whenever, I come to Delhi from Lucknow, I experience a dual feeling of joy and nostalgia when my mother pampers me with love as my grandmother did for her son. In today's hectic and fast paced life there is hardly time for savouring maternal love and bonding.

My grandmother lived only for nine months after the demise of Babuji. Those nine months were a tortuous time for her. She used to hold Babuji's photograph and keep talking to it as though Babuji were alive. Whenever I went near her, she would say: "… this Nanhe (my son) had given me lots of trouble for nine months in my womb before coming into the world, but I didn't know that he would leave this world troubling me for another nine months." She died exactly nine months later making me wonder how she anticipated her death in nine months so precisely.

A few days before her death, I had secured a job as an apprentice with the Bank of India. Those were days of shock, grief and bewilderment as Babuji's sudden death had plunged the family into an economic and psychological crisis. I had still to complete my studies but I felt that I had

▲ To grandpa with love

to do my bit to support the family. I decided to take up the bank job and along side working complete my studies. One Saturday when I returned home from work, I was startled to hear my grandmother's voice: "Nanhe, have you come?" The repetition of those lines in her familiar soft voice drew me to her. Seeing me she said "Oh! Mohan Krishna", (that is how she used to call me) "it is you?" She kissed me and patted me the same way she did with Babuji and I asked her why she called out to me as "Nanhe". She replied: "I don't know why I felt that Nanhe had returned."

I got my first month's salary of ₹ 430 and I bought two khadi sarees, one for my mother and the other for grandma. I kept them at her feet and received her blessings.

My maternal grand parents lived in Chetganj, a small Mohalla in Mirzapur I had not seen Nana, but I remember Nani and visits to her house as beautiful memories ever present in my mind. But I was disturbed by the underdeveloped state of the town that had remained so for many years since pre-independence days. The life style of the town was pathetic and there was no effort, leave aside desire, on their part to raise their standard of living. It is beyond my understanding as to why these people never venture to get out of their fossilized state and move ahead with times. A simple example will illustrate the mindset of the town who hold on to archaic customs and

traditions without ever knowing why they do so. My Nani was always addressed as Mava and when I asked Amma why she was so called, she said she had no clue to it. She just followed her elder brother and sisters who used Mava in place of Amma or Ma to address her. No one had ever tried to understand or question why they did so. This is true of most villages who make a habit of custom without questioning. This is so different from modern perceptions that value "examined life" so well popularized in Greece by Socrates nearly 2500 years ago. Implicit obedience amounting to abject surrender to old customs has been the root cause of our rural underdevelopment. In small villages a boy's uncle often becomes everybody's uncle and a son-in-law becomes everybody's son-in-law and in course of time, it becomes an accepted fact.

Babuji was likewise the illustrious son-in-law of Chetganj. He loved visiting my uncle Chandrika Prasad with whom he shared a great rapport. During his visit to my uncle's house after he became Prime Minister, he was just his previous unassuming self-laughing, chatting and mixing with everyone like a member of their family. I was young and I couldn't believe that Babuji, the Prime Minister could behave and move like a common man. He carried his greatness so light on his shoulders. Babuji had a twin relationship with Mirzapur—he was both the son-

◀ Shastriji and Sunil.

in-law of the place as well as its grandson as his maternal grandfather's house was also in the same area.

I was curious to know how Amma accepted Babuji who from his youthful days had pledged his life for the service of the nation and had become a part of the Freedom movement. Amma told me that she had also been brought on the ideals of patriotism from her childhood. She said: When I met Babuji for the first time, I was 9–10 years old. There had been a death in our neighbourhood. My mother had to go there and she asked us not to leave the house. Out of curiosity, my sister and I peeped out to see what was happening in that house. Shastriji was among the people present at that place. He was silent and looked lost in his world. All of a sudden I said: "Everyone is crying but Dulari Behen's son is not crying." Ram Dulari Behen was later to become my Amma's mother-in-law). "Later, whenever, I recalled these words, I would burst into laughter. My mind at that time equated silence with insensitivity and crying with sadness. My mother was keen to have Shastriji as her son-in-law. She wanted my elder sister to be married to Shastriji, but then his mother Mava was not ready for it. Two years later she revived the subject to her brother. There were a few prospective matches on hand, but luckily for me they all failed. Personally, I wanted only Shastriji and I fasted and prayed for it to materialize. I also dreamt that I met him at the precincts of a temple and I put a garland around his neck while he gave me a bouquet of flowers." Amma's tapasya was like Meera's for Lord Krishna and the consummation of their marriage almost had a divine quality. Like Meera Bai, Amma had also brought home one of God's images from a nearby temple without anyone's knowledge. She used to pray like Meera Bai so that she would be united only with Shastriji. But when her Bhaiya began pursuing other matches, she dropped the image of God into water saying "When you have decided to drown me, I will also drown you in water." But when my Bhaiya reported to my mother that all those alliances he was pursuing had failed, I quietly went out and took the image from water and thanked God for his kindness. Nearly a year had passed when again my Bhaiya found yet another prospective match with a well to do family in Benares. Everyone except me was excited. Again I drowned the image in water and decided to drown myself. Thank God, Bhaiya returned home from Benares, disappointed with the boy and I was on cloud nine. I took the image out of water and bent down in obeisance again and again.

That was when Shastriji's mother come and took a token of one rupee and a roll of cloth to conclude the alliance. On the 9th May, 1928, Shastriji was sent a telegram to proceed to Benares. He came to know of his wedding after reaching Benares. He was surprised and told his mother that she should have at least asked him once before finalising it. Anyhow since his mother had decided, he said that he would abide by her wishes. The marriage took place a week later.

Unlike in the West where the Prime Minister's wife is given special position and respect as 'the First Lady of the Nation', here in India, she enjoys no such status. In the case of Amma, after the demise of Babuji, she did not figure in the minds of the people. I say this with sadness not because she was my mother, but that she truly symbolized the soul of India. She was a unique person who was ever willing to stay in the background even when her husband was numero uno in the country. She never asked for the status of the 'First lady' and she stayed at home, relieving Babuji of family worries. It is in this sense she was the true woman of India playing multiple roles as wife, mother, daughter-in-law, home-maker and last but not the least a companion to her husband sharing his tension and anxieties and caring for him and for the nation.

When I was born my father became the Police Minister of Uttar Pradesh. Amma brought me to her mother who was old and with declining vision. She was happy to see me, a fair and healthy baby who she felt had brought luck to his father. "Ever since he arrived, his father became the Police Minister. You will see, one day he will go to great heights and his father, of course will continue climbing the ladder of success." Her clairvoyance did come true in the case of Babuji who later became the Prime Minister of India. As for me, I hope it proves equally true especially if I become a worthy son of a worthy father.

Whatever Nani said had happened. I became the Deputy Minister of Uttar Pradesh. My only aim all my life has been to do my best in the service of my people. Babuji had sown the seeds of social welfare and social service in me. The seeds had sprouted and become saplings when I went to Madhya Pradesh at the tender age of 16. Now the saplings have grown into plants and in course of time with my journey through life, I expect them to grow into trees and provide sustenance and shelter to all those who come near it. If Nani's predictions were to come true, I will achieve the goal I had set out to achieve from my teenage.

My knowledge about Babuji was limited to my early years when he had become the Prime Minister. I hardly knew Babuji's younger days when he had joined the Satyagraha movement launched by Gandhiji and was imprisoned by the British government. I learnt much later from Amma about Babuji's participation in the Freedom struggle, his defiance of the Martial Law imposed by the

British and his consequent incarceration. Though Amma did not remember all the details, she could recollect Babuji's stubbornness to join the volunteer's group that went to Sholapur where Martial law had been in force. He wouldn't listen even to Rajshree Purushottam Das Tandon, a highly respected leader who advised him not to risk his life by going there. Finding him adamant in his resolve, Tandonji asked Amma to stop her husband on this dangerous expedition. Since she knew that she could never convince Babuji to change his decision, she approached Babuji's mother to exert maternal pressure on her son. My grandmother heard her daughter-in-law and remained silent for a while. Then quietly she said: "No, I can't stop my son from going there. When he has put his step forward, it is not correct to ask him to retract. Whatever happens will be God's wish." Babuji's mother was a person of great strength and courage. Babuji must have inherited all these qualities from her—indomitable courage to shoulder responsibility, steely strength to face hardships and never to retract after taking a principled stand.

She knew her son very well and hence she refused to interfere with his decisions.

But Amma decided in a different way. Instead of asking her husband not to go to Sholapur, she asked him to take her also with him. Babuji questioned her: " What will you do there? You must be here to take care of Amma" (his mother). Amma in turn was adamant and said: "No, I will not stay here alone. I will go wherever you go." Babuji quietly put a full stop to my plea saying: "No, this is not possible" I started crying and for once Babuji lost his cool and sternly said: "If you had abused me even then that would not have been so painful as these words of yours. I will often have to participate in work like this. Where all can I take you?" Finally he said that he will not go to Sholapur this time on condition that I promised never to interfere in future with his work. I made the promise and I kept my word till the end. In a sad tone Amma added that this promise kept her away from him during his tragic visit to Tashkent—an eternal regret to her.

Amma's eyes were full of pain and agony. But shining through her misty eyes was the simple, honest woman who played a quiet supportive role in all her husband's decisions and activities. She was truly the First Lady of the Nation, never pushing herself forward to be feted and honoured, but always in the background, sacrificing her needs and her demands on his time so that he could attend to the demands of his office with a free and peaceful mind. Babuji, for her was first Prime Minister and then her husband. Not many have appreciated the quiet role she had played in the success of her husband. That is the way of the world, where glitter and glamour take precedence over a wife's quiet and caring role. Years later in 1987, more than two decades after the death of her husband, talks were on to make her contest from Allahabad. She had been India's unacknowledged First Lady, the wife of a former Prime Minister and she did not want to return to politics in the absence of a mentor like her husband. Amma was a personification of dignity, nobility and simplicity. Having lost the most precious of her possessions, she did not desire any new status.

Amma recalled the days when Babuji was arrested for participating in the Salt Satyagraha movement. He had earlier asked them not to cry and make a scene if he went to jail. "Maybe I will have to go to jail in a few days but if anybody cries on my going to prison, I will think that he or she does not love me much. The one who truly loves me will not shed even a drop of tear."

"Maybe I will have to go to jail in a few days but if anybody cries on my going to prison, I will think that he or she does not love me much. The one who truly loves me will not shed even a drop of tear."

Amma added: "Babuji did not tell me that he was going to break the Salt Law. He had not returned till late in the evening. I was getting restless and worried. I went up the terrace to see if he was anywhere in the vicinity. I saw a lorry with a hoard of arrested freedom fighters shouting

"Inqalab Zindabad. Gandhiji ki jai". I could see Babuji among them. He waved his hands when he saw me. I kept staring at him. The lorry sped away. My eyes were full of tears, but I remembered his words: "Person who would cry would love me less". I wiped my tears but doubts assailed me if it was Shastriji whom I saw. But then he had waved to me and who else could it be except Shastriji. When his mother came home, I informed her of her son's arrest. I was tense as it was his first imprisonment but did not cry as per his wishes. Around 11'O clock, there was a knock on the door. Babuji had sent word that he had gone to jail.

Amma's stoic acceptance, her inner strength to defy grief, her respect for Babuji's wishes made a strong impact on me. She represented the many women of her generation who had sacrificed their family happiness for the sake of their nation's independence. Men went to jail, but women suffered within the four walls of their homes. They suffered, but they did not lament or cry. Their grief gave them strength and their contribution to the freedom struggle was in no way less than that of their husbands. I kissed Amma and touched her feet in awe and reverence. Her indomitable spirit was the sustaining force during those sad days after the demise of Babuji.

Amma's life story with all its ups and downs has been an object lesson for me. She was a woman with grit and determination to prove worthy of her husband. She had no formal education as sending girls to school in those days was not considered auspicious. When she was with Babuji in Allahabad, she sought the help of her Bengali neighbour who was good at Hindi to learn the language. As for payment of fees, she decided to save on the maid's salary Lapart-time lady cleaning the flour and utensils by doing the household chores herself and spend it on her tuition. Though Babuji was happy about her decision to learn Hindi, he was also concerned about her health as it meant a heavy schedule for her both mentally and physically. Amma assured him that she would be mindful of her health and that studies were important for her to spare him any kind of discomfiture on account of her illiteracy. Babuji's silence meant a quiet nod for his wife's decision.

Babuji was a man of few words. But there were times when his words had a strong effect on his listeners. His "Jai Jawan, Jai Kisan" is a good example of his great felicity with words. Amma once told me that a year after his return from jail, he came home. His knock was familiar and Amma ran to open the door. Instead of Babuji, she saw a stranger in a scout's uniform and before she could close the door on him he had entered the house. His mother was also startled to see a stranger barging into the house. It was a little while before they realized it was Babuji in a different outfit. He said that he wanted to test how brave his wife was. Amma told him that she was not a coward and that she would have faced any threat if she had not been taken by surprise. Babuji who was by nature not given to argument to score brownie points told her: "Danger never informs you of its arrival; it just comes. Man should always be ready to face it all the time, only then he can gain victory over it" wise words truthfully said. Amma remembered these words all her life. Life's uncertainty does take everyone by surprise. But to succumb to it in fear and desperation is an act of cowardice. Amma had to face such shocks in her life. First was Babuji's sudden death at Tashkent. Then she lost her eldest daughter and later youngest son, my younger brother. This was a big blow to her. To accept this third loss needed nerves of steel. Amma did not allow the tragedy to destroy her and the rest of the family. Like a strong matriarch, she showed the way to all of us to face the tragedy with dignity and courage. Her grief was immense; so was her stoic acceptance. To her loss and gain were two sides of the same coin. She understood the fact of life, sometimes we win, other times we lose. But we can never predict the outcome of the toss of the coin. Heads or tails, we have to accept with equanimity.

"Danger never informs you of its arrival; it just comes. Man should always be ready to face it all the time, only then he can gain victory over it"

An example of Amma's endurance of grief without making an exhibition of it is the way she handled crass, insensitive questions of press reporters soon after Babuji's death. One of them asked her: "Now, after being Prime Minister's wife how do you feel?" The question sounded bizarre as though the grief of a Prime Minister's wife could be different. Amma calmly replied: "I don't feel anything but when people like you come and ask such questions, then I realize that there must be something special in me now, because earlier none of you visited us before." I don't know whether the reporter realized that he was talking to someone special whose great grief was matched by greater endurance. Babuji's influence on Amma was such that she had become another edition of Babuji—gentle and firm, emotional and rational, philosophical and practical, humane and spiritual with no clash between the juxtaposed contraries.

I had also learnt a lot from Babuji. Babuji was the Home Minister (the Police Minister) of Uttar Pradesh, when I was born I used to imagine having a big luxury car commensurate with the status of Babuji. It did happen when Babuji became the Prime Minister. He was given a Chevrolet

Impala for his official use. As PM's sons my brother Anil and I developed the habit of ordering officials to do my bidding. One day I told Babuji's personal secretary to ask the driver to bring the Chevrolet to the residence. We asked the driver for the keys and went for a drive. We went to a place where we had a dinner appointment. We ate and talked and lost track of time. We realized that Babuji must have returned home and would be upset if we had used the official vehicle for our personal use. I stopped the car in front of the gate and quietly entered the house from the kitchen side. Just as I entered, I met Amma and I asked her if Babuji had returned and whether he asked for anything in particular. She nodded in the affirmative and I did not

have the courage to ask what he had enquired. I told her that since I was sleeping late, I should not be disturbed early in the morning. My clever thinking was if I did not surface before Babuji, he might forget to enquire about the car.

Around 6:30 in the morning, there was a knock on my door. Thinking it would be some servant with bed tea, I said in a high pitched voice not to disturb me as I had retired to bed late at night. But there was a knock again and reluctantly I got up to see Babuji standing. I apologized to him for my delay in opening the door and he, as usual unruffled, said that he didn't mind it and would wait for me to have a cup of tea.

I soon got ready and joined him at the table. He didn't ask me anything and it made me wonder whether he knew about our soiree at dinner time the previous day. Amma, on the other hand, asked me point blank as to where we had gone and why we got late to return home. When I said that we had gone out for dinner, Babuji asked me: "How did you go? When I came I saw the fiat (his personal car) parked under the tree. I had to tell the truth about our drive in the Impala Chevorlet. Babuji seldom used this big car except when state guests came. Again without showing any sign of anger he said: "Aha! You boys like driving a big luxurious car." I signalled to Anil bhaiya that Babuji had almost given the green signal for us to use that car whenever we wanted it. After finishing his tea, he asked me to call the driver in. He asked him;" Do you keep a log book with you?" When he nodded, Babuji asked him to note the distance the car had run the previous day. When the driver said "14 kms" he advised him to note it 'for private use' and then asked Amma to give his personal secretary the amount rate applicable as per km for 14 kms to be deposited in the government account. Both Anil bhaiya and I were in tears. There was no harsh exchange from Babuji and in his gentle way he had pointed to our mistake. To this day, my brother and I who are in active politics have not misused the official perks that come with office. Very often my boys complain that I send them to school either by a rickshaw or on a bicycle while many students come in their father's government cars. It is difficult to convince them about the merits of honesty to the smallest detail, but Babuji had given us lessons for life without the need for debate or discussion. His actions spoke for his integrity and honesty. In these days of corruption and dishonest practices, Babuji's mentoring has sustained us on the path of absolute rectitude.

He was more a friend and a guide than a father. His life was an open book for us to savour and follow. He used to ask me and my brother to attend to some of his personal work. We were proud to do his work.

There was always a competition between the two of us as to who does the most for Babuji and how well he does it. One day Babuji asked me to arrange his cupboard and clean his room. I did it with great care and happiness. Next day Babuji complimented me for the work I had done and asked me where had I kept his three kurtas. I answered that they were torn (one near the collar, the other under the arm and the third near the pocket) and so I had handed them to Amma. It was the last week of October. Babuji said that it will be winter soon and that he could wear the torn kurtas under his coat. These kurtas, he continued, were Khadi kurtas made with a lot of labour and care. Hence they should not be discarded till every fibre of it had been utilized. That was the first time I understood how Babuji lived a modest and frugal life. He often handed over his kurtas to Amma, when they became totally unusable and asked her to make handkerchiefs out of them. He lived on the simple philosophy of 'waste not, want not'. It is often said as a joke that a garbage bin in the US is worth many thousand dollars. Today, we are least mindful of wasting huge quantities of food during parties and marriages. We seem to follow the American trend throwing out the country's resources that would feed a thousand hungry. Babuji had demonstrated to me the need to conserve the nation's resources. It is a well-known saying that great things come in small packages. Babuji illustrated this throughout his life. A man of small stature with a big and generous heart, Babuji personified the true Gandhian qualities of simplicity, modesty, care and concern for all those who were not privileged to have a modicum of comfort in their lives. He never preached morals or philosophy but lived them. Those of us who were close to him were inspired by the ideals he stood for. I also began to love khadi though Babuji never asked me to wear it.

Amma once told me that she had at the time of her marriage received just five pieces of jewellery. Babuji asked for them when his uncle had suffered a heavy financial loss. "Though initially I hesitated, I gave him all that I had except three small essential pieces that a married woman had to wear. The next day Babuji asked me what would be my reply if people were to ask about the rest of your jewellery. I answered him that following Gandhiji's advice I had stopped wearing jewellery. Moreover I have the real jewellery with me—the vermillion mark on my forehead, my bangles and my nose ring. I do not need anything more. Life has its vicissitudes and one has to accept them. What is up today will go down tomorrow but what is down tomorrow will rise again the following day."

Amma had her share of ups and downs. With Babujis' death, she gave up wearing two of the three symbols of a married woman—the vermillion mark and bangles. She continued wearing the nose ring and when foolish and insensitive people objected, she firmly said: "he made me wear this; it will go along with me." Amma once told me the significance of the nose ring. She had accompanied Babuji on a visit to Madras after he had become the Prime Minister. The tradition down south was that almost all women wore nose rings. They suggested to me that I could wear a nose ring with diamond as it might go well with me. I was quite excited and requested Babuji to get a diamond nose ring ready for me.

He was surprised at my childish request and said that he would get one for me though I should not harbour such immature desires. I regretted my foolishness and told him not to get me the diamond nose ring. We returned to Delhi and the incident was forgotten. After many days, when I was getting his lunch ready, Babuji called me from the kitchen and placed a diamond nose ring in my hand. Hence her resolve to wear it for life.

Looking at the different facets of Amma's life—bride, wife, daughter-in-law, mother, mother-in-law and the final phase when she lost her husband I see her as an extension of my Dadi. In today's world, saas–bahu relationships have changed vastly. In those days in India, the words of a mother-in-law were sacrosanct. Amma never disobeyed her mother-in-law's wishes and advice. Dadi was far more modern in her outlook for that age. Those were the days when meetings, pickettings and sacrifices were a part of the satyagraha movement. Men and women spontaneously joined the movement launched by Gandhiji. Dadi took Amma to the various meetings addressed by great leaders of that time. She also encouraged her daughter-in-law to go with her son to these meetings. Her only insistence was that Amma kept her face covered. Amma knew that for Babuji, his mother's word was final and so Amma respected Dadi's instructions without a protest.

Though Babuji wanted his wife to take part in the picketing movement against foreign goods, his mother did not agree saying a woman's place was first and foremost at home and all outside matters for her should be secondary. Babuji didn't agree but as a true son, he accepted her dictum. When Nehruji's wife, Kamalaji asked Babuji as to why he did not permit his wife to participate, he diplomatically said that he had not been able to convince his wife, but she may agree if Kamalaji spoke to her. He knew that his mother could never refuse Kamalaji and that happened. Dadi, in response to Kamalaji's request agreed to Amma's participation in picketing. Since Amma had no clue what was to be done, she sought Babuji's advice. He told her to stand calmly in front of the shops that sold foreign goods and politely dissuade those who came to buy them. Amma said that she along with her neighbour went to a shop selling foreign clothes and urged people, mainly women not to buy them. Their duty was for two hours starting mid-day, but before long they discovered that someone mischievously had set fire to a shop next door. There was chaos and stampede all around. Her friend said that it would be prudent to leave the place. Amma was also scared, though she thought that Babuji would be annoyed if they abandoned their duty before time. Since her friend was not ready to stay longer, Amma also returned home with her. But the very next day, her confidence had increased and Amma could convincingly persuade people not to buy the foreign stuff. The shopkeeper was getting irritated and told her that the bangles she was wearing were also of foreign origin. Her friend remonstrated that his watch was also foreign made. Amma was quick to seize an opportunity that unfolded before her. She told him that if she broke her bangles—something no married woman will ever do, he should also break his watch.The shopkeeper agreed on the strength of his belief that Amma would not break her bangles as it was inauspicious. Babuji who had then arrived there gave her the signal to break. Amma did so but when the shopkeeper hesitated to do the same, those who had come for shopping got annoyed and left. One of the buyers set fire to the clothes he had purchased and set the shop also on fire.

On returning home, Amma had to face her mother-in-law who would have disapproved of her action. Amma made some clever excuse to assuage her anxiety. This incident that Amma narrated to me made a lasting impact on my mind. Amma was one of a rare kind who had the wisdom, maturity and courage to act in national interest even if that action meant defiance of tradition. For Amma, a pious person, though not literate, all irrational traditional practices (such as breaking bangles on the demise of the husband) in the name of religion are arguable and disputable. It is wrong to justify superstitious beliefs in the name of tradition as that would mean abdicating one's rationality. In her quiet way this act of hers showed her mature awareness of the crimes committed against women in the name of tradition and religion.

Amma has been a mentor to me. Everytime I experienced a dilemma, I had sought her advice. When I had to take the difficult decision of resigning as minister in the government of Uttar Pradesh, Amma showed me what was right. She told me: "You have been born and brought up as a Congress man. You have no individual identity other than what Congress has given you. That identity is not to be bartered for position and power. It is self-respect that is important rather than office." Amma was as much of a wise counsellor as Babuji used to be. As a politician and as a true bred Congress man—I uphold these valuable words of Amma. Babuji had lived a life of simplicity, nobility and dignity and had put the nation before self. He rose to be the Prime Minister despite being a common man with all the limitations it imposed on one's upbringing. But he proved capable and worthy of the position conferred upon him. Babuji was indeed a unique person with special qualities of being authentically human.

Babuji's political career spanned more than four decades. His early years were spent in jail during the freedom movement. Soon after Independence and before the Constitution was made, there was an interim government. Babuji who had come out of jail was summoned by the then Prime minister of United Province Pantji to come to Lucknow. Amma was somewhat disturbed as she needed him to stay back in Allahabad. Babuji told her that she need not worry as he would earn enough to manage the family. Amma told him that she was not bothered about herself as her happiness was where he was, but only about the children whom she had brought up with real difficulty when he was in jail.

Babuji had never asked for any personal favour or help during his entire political career. With the little money he gave to his wife, she had looked after her children and her mother-in-law. Babuji always gave credit to his wife who accepted a difficult and frugal living without complaint. She had great faith in Babuji that he had the qualities to rise up to high position. On the strength of her confidence in her husband's abilities, she made her children study and not to go in search of small jobs for the sake of money. We didn't have much to eat or live comfortably, but we were full of contentment and happiness with what little there was in the house.

In today's world where greed has replaced need, there is no place for simple living. The wheel of progress has moved in the opposite direction where frugality is mocked at and where quality of life is measured by money and not by happiness. In today's context it is difficult even to understand, leave aside appreciate Babuji's simplicity. Even after holding the highest position in the Government, Babuji remained the same simple khadi wearing person and wore his old torn kurtas beneath his coat during winter. He was a spotlessly clean man—both in personal appearance and in his professional engagements. He could not stand dirt in his premises and if he found papers strewn here and there by us, he would stoop down to pick them up. He was the Prime Minister in office feted and revered, but returning home, he preferred doing things by himself. Neither Amma nor the servants dared to interfere with his

▼ Shastriji in Burma

▲ Talking to visitors (Shastriji: Open house)

▼ 1. Shastriji with Congress leaders
2. Nehru, Krishna Menon and Shastriji

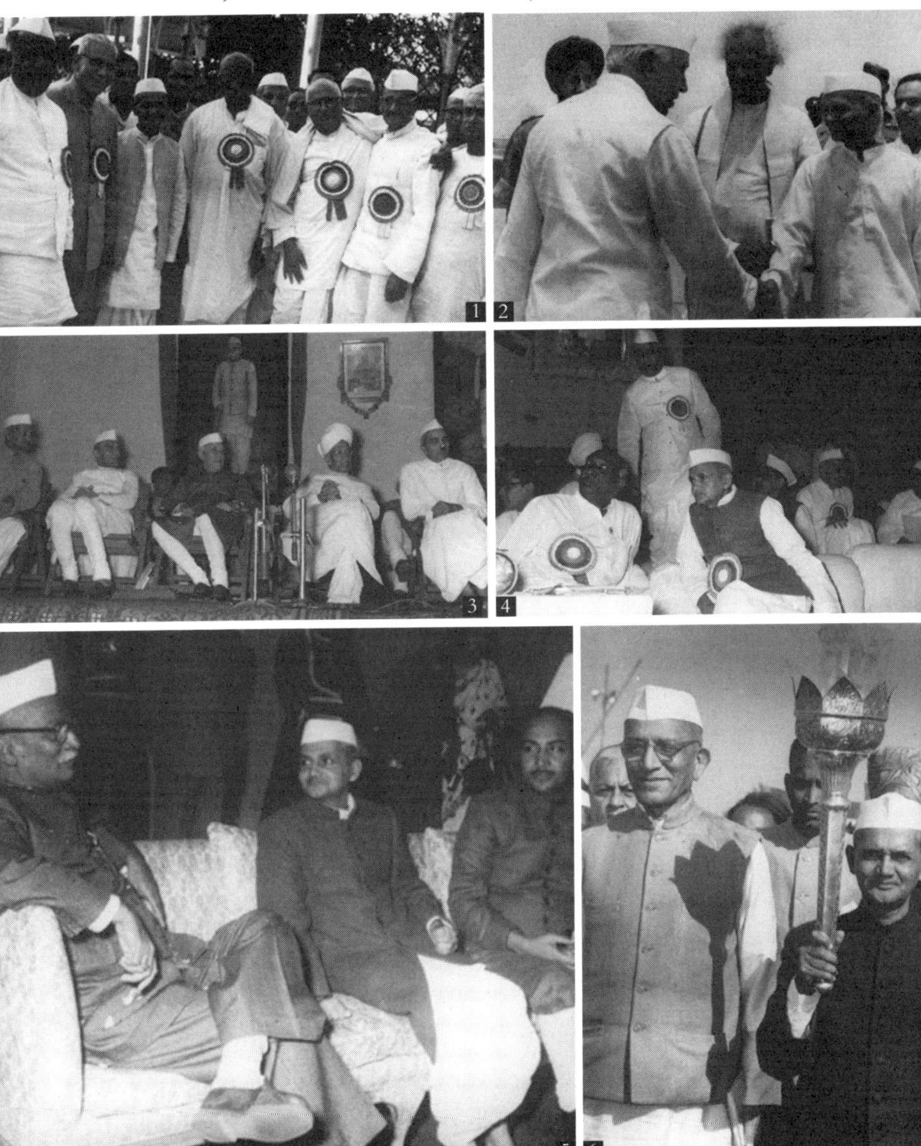

▲ 3. Shastriji with Radha Krishnan 4. With Kamraj
5. With Rajendra Prasad 6. With Morarji Desai

work and stood helpless and embarrassed before the little big man's selfless humility.

In this way he taught us the value of self-help, humility and dignity of labour. He never let lose his temper on the servants even if they committed a big offence. Once because of his servant's carelessness, the box he had to take with him was misplaced and as a result his flight got delayed by half an hour. He didn't question the servant as to how this mistake was committed but his silence said it all. The servant was left wondering what his master thought of him as he never revealed his annoyance at any time. The happiness and welfare of others mattered most to him and he was a role model of a selfless and untiring worker. The happiness and pleasure he got in making others happy was indescribable.

Babuji never wanted personal comforts specially given to him that were not made available for the common people. When he was the Minister for Railways, he travelled in the first class coach as per his entitlement. Once during summer when he took the train journey to Mumbai (in those days, it was called Bombay), he realized that it was quite cool inside the compartment while outside it was blazing hot. His personal assistant, Kailash Babu informed him that there was an ice brick kept which made the coach cool. Babuji was upset that while the other passengers travelled in the hot weather, his journey was made comfortable. He asked his P.A. "Why did you not consult me before keeping the ice brick? Are the other people travelling in this train not human? Actually I should be travelling in the third class, since that is not possible, whatever is possible should be done that makes me one of them. Wherever the train stops, please remove the ice brick." Today, we come across phrases like 'cattle class', as distinct from the premier classes. Babuji, in true Gandhian style preferred to travel like a commoner without the perks attached to the Railway Minister. The ice brick was removed at the next station. He lived according to his principles. He never preached but he lived all those values he had stood for. He was always one with his people and never allowed anyone to make a special distinction for his sake. He remembered that he had risen from amongst them and he passed on that sense and value to me. He had sent me to Madhya Pradesh rural area when I was fifteen to learn their way of living, to understand them and to live with them. I carry within me the values that he lived by. I had the good fortune to see him practise these values everyday in every aspect of his life and I carry his value-laden baton as my precious heritage.

Amma was a perfect foil to Babuji. They were made for each other. Babuji was the modern Karna—ever ready to extend a helping hand to whosoever in distress. He would turn to Amma to give him whatever money she had with her so that he could help people with their financial problems. Amma told me that whenever she saw Babuji coming with his cap on one hand and scratching his head with the other, she knew he needed money. She used to call her daughter standing near her and softly say, "See now, Babuji is about to ask for money." Babuji would start with a detailed account of the difficulties of the person concerned and then request her for money to be given to him. "Somebody's problems would be solved with your money; somebody would be able to smile because of you." Babuji's gentle persuasiveness was always the key to his winning ways. His kindness, his altruism, his faith in his wife's generosity and his genuine concern for other's problems were unique and till the end he acted selflessly in the interest of all who approached him. Amma and Babuji enjoyed excellent rapport with each other. They had a perfect understanding of one other's needs and acted in tandem to serve the people. Their mutual co-operation was in evidence in everything they did together in their social, political and family life. The way they complemented each other can be seen in the following example.

"Somebody's problems would be solved with your money"

Prior to our independence, Babuji was asked by Nehruji to take charge of all the correspondence addressed to him. There was mutual trust between them and Nehruji discussed various issues with him. Once Nehruji sought Babuji's advice regarding a letter wherein the writer said that he doubted the loyalty of his wife. Nehruji placed the letter in front of Babuji and asked him as to what he should reply. Babuji was uncomfortable with this personal issue between a husband and wife, but Nehruji insisted on Babuji discussing it with his wife and getting back to him with her response. Babuji brought the letter home and discussed it with her. Amma politely told him: "Whatever you think about me, write the same in your reply. That gentleman's problem will be solved." Babuji did exactly as she said. Between Amma and Babuji, there was absolute trust and there was no room for doubt to smudge that beautiful relationship. Their life founded on mutual faith and respect is an object lesson for all married people.

Babuji's political ascendance was well merited. He moved from Railway Ministry to Communication and Transport to Commerce and Industry to become the Home Minister of India—a position next to the Prime Minister. Amma's prayers played no less a significant role in Babuji's success. She prayed for hours for Babuji's success as he had to shoulder the responsibility of the nation and affirm its dignity and integrity so well nurtured by Panditji.

Panditji's sudden death was a big shock to the nation. For Babuji, it was a personal and irreparable loss and all of a sudden the mantle had fallen on him. He needed God's grace to help him shoulder the huge responsibility of leading the Nation. Amma spent most of her time praying and seeking God's blessings on him in his discharge of his duties and responsibilities.

Babuji had always been a tireless and selfless worker. The hours he worked as Prime Minister were the same when he worked as the Police Minister of Uttar Pradesh and earlier as an organizational worker of the Congress party in the pre-independence days.

Babuji had a special ability for trouble shooting and could solve all tricky issues without causing offence or distress to anyone. He was an adept in bringing round the opposition to his point of view and would settle all differences in a unique and amicable way. He was never a part of any controversy because he had no personal interest or selfish agenda on any issue. He was a true Gandhian and he lived by the principles of Gandhiji all his life. Work was never a burden to him and he was in every sense of the term a people's person—selfless, honest, gentle, wisely persuasive and principled.

Amma gave me an example of Babuji's uprightness; When he was in Faizabad jail, Amma visited him there covertly carrying with her two mangoes, Babuji's favourite fruit. As per the jail manual, no eatable was to be taken inside the jail to be given to the prisoner. Amma wanted to personally give him the fruit. She could take the mangoes in without being noticed. When she placed the mangoes before Babuji, he became furious and said: "Since you have brought them stealthily and against the jail injunctions, I will not touch them. I will also ask the jail warden how you were allowed to bring these mangoes slyly." He chastised her saying that her action smacked of selfishness as she didn't want to be deprived of eating mangoes herself without her husband tasting them. Amma was saddened at his outburst. Babuji refused to talk to her while he was his normal gentle self with the other visitors.

But true to his nature, after a few days, he wrote a letter of apology to Amma for his bad behaviour. That was the greatness of this little man. Even when he was angry for the right reason, he was quick to realize that he had erred on appreciating Amma's emotions and sought her forgiveness. Nobility, thy name is Lal Bahadur Shastri.

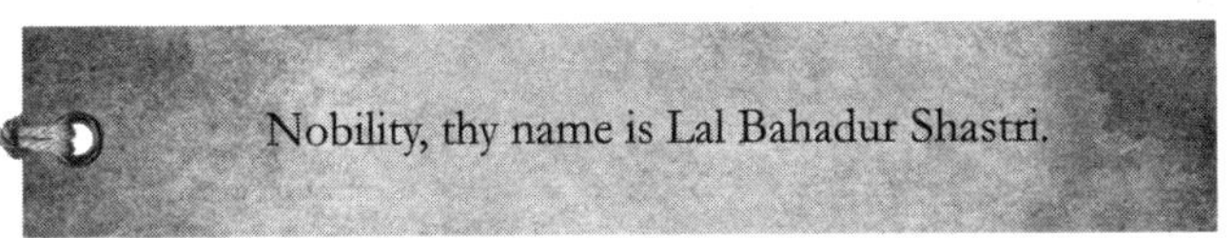

Babuji worked hard at every opportunity and deserved all that he had attained in life. His reaching great heights were not just a matter of luck or destiny. He never asked for anything, but when some ministerial position was offered to him, he was ready to use that opportunity to work for the betterment of his people. From his childhood, he had practised the virtues of honesty, selflessness and simplicity. When he was elevated to the big offices, he carried with him all the virtues he had in his genes. Till date there has not been a systematic and objective assessment of Babuji's work, but whenever it happens in the future, it may throw light on the genetic characteristics of Babuji who could be both a Prime Minister and a common man

▲ Shastriji leaving for Tashkent - The last live journey

at the same time. The mighty offices did not change his natural personality nor his rise from the ranks affect his Prime Ministerial functions. His transition to the highest office was without any fear or trepidation or fanfare as he was essentially a human being.

When I talk about Babuji, I primarily recall his essential roots as a human being. He has in a way passed on these roots to me. In this new world where ostentation, glamour and luxury are the buzz words I feel a strange sense of alienation. When I was the Power Minister of Uttar Pradesh, my office was on the 12th floor of Shakti Bhavan. From that height, I could view the whole city of Lucknow. Once after a high level meeting with executives and officers of the power board, I was alone in my room looking out of the window at the cityscape. The plush ambience of my office was in stark contrast to my modest upbringing among common people most of whom live on streets and lanes dotting the city. I had moved with the masses from my early days and I related to them as I related to my family. Standing alone on this high raised building, I felt a strange sense of loneliness and emptiness, not dissimilar to what Gautam Buddha must have felt on witnessing human suffering among his people, their poverty and illness, their life of misery and death. Buddha, as we all know, renounced everything and went in search of finding the truth.

But I get deeply disturbed at the idea of renunciation. Whenever I speak about my mixed feelings of service to the nation through holding office and giving up everything to be with ordinary common men and women, no one ever understands me with the exception of Meera, my wife and my mother. I find it difficult to open up before the new generation who make fun of my idea of renunciation of worldly prestige and position to involve myself with simple and humble people in villages and remote areas of the country. Gandhiji remarked that India lives in her villages. I fully understand his pertinent observation. The pure and pristine Indian soul exists in the villages where people live, honest and simple life in an environment that contributes to mental and physical health in full measure. Even when I stood on the 12th floor of my ministerial office, I longed for my childhood days of innocence and joy, my early days in humble and happy surroundings.

I always loved that atmosphere, uncluttered by the chaos and stress of the mega cities and towns where need is replaced by greed, silence by noise, purity by pollution and fellow feeling by self-centredness. I was young when Babuji as a Minister had become a part of the government. We lived in luxury in an official bungalow with official cars and high ranking officers frequenting the house. I could have lapped up all these luxuries and asserted my right to anything and everything as the minister's son. But somehow I was brought up differently. I was in fact wary of all these frills that come with ministership. I discerned the emptiness behind all this pomp and show and this was due to the Spartan atmosphere in our house. Amma and Babuji as well as my sisters Kusum didi and Suman didi were deeply linked to the roots of life. For them the surface glamour had no meaning. They drew their sustenance from the core of life behind all the glittering paraphernalia that official status brings with it. Their influence on me was of a lasting kind as I recognized the ephemeral nature of worldly glamour and the emptiness at its core. I had not known or seen Babuji's simple family life. I had only seen the brighter period of his life when he was successful and respected as a leader of the nation. But what has abided with me is that he was essentially a man of the masses who followed what he believed in—a life of service and simplicity. As I stood near the window of my office on the 12th floor of Shakti Bhavan, I felt the need to renew my energy—my shakti from my roots. Abraham Lincoln, former President of the US said:

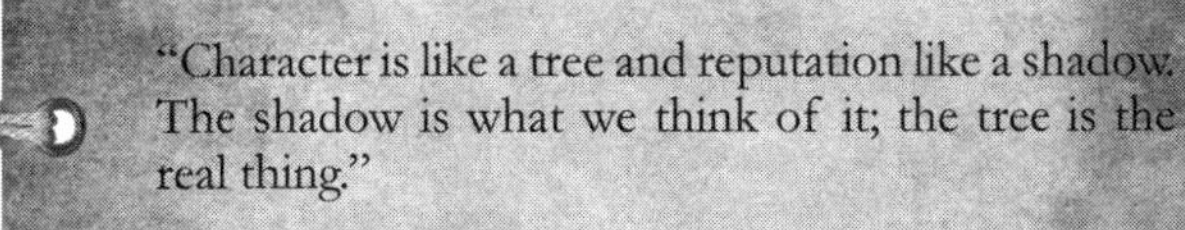

"Character is like a tree and reputation like a shadow. The shadow is what we think of it; the tree is the real thing."

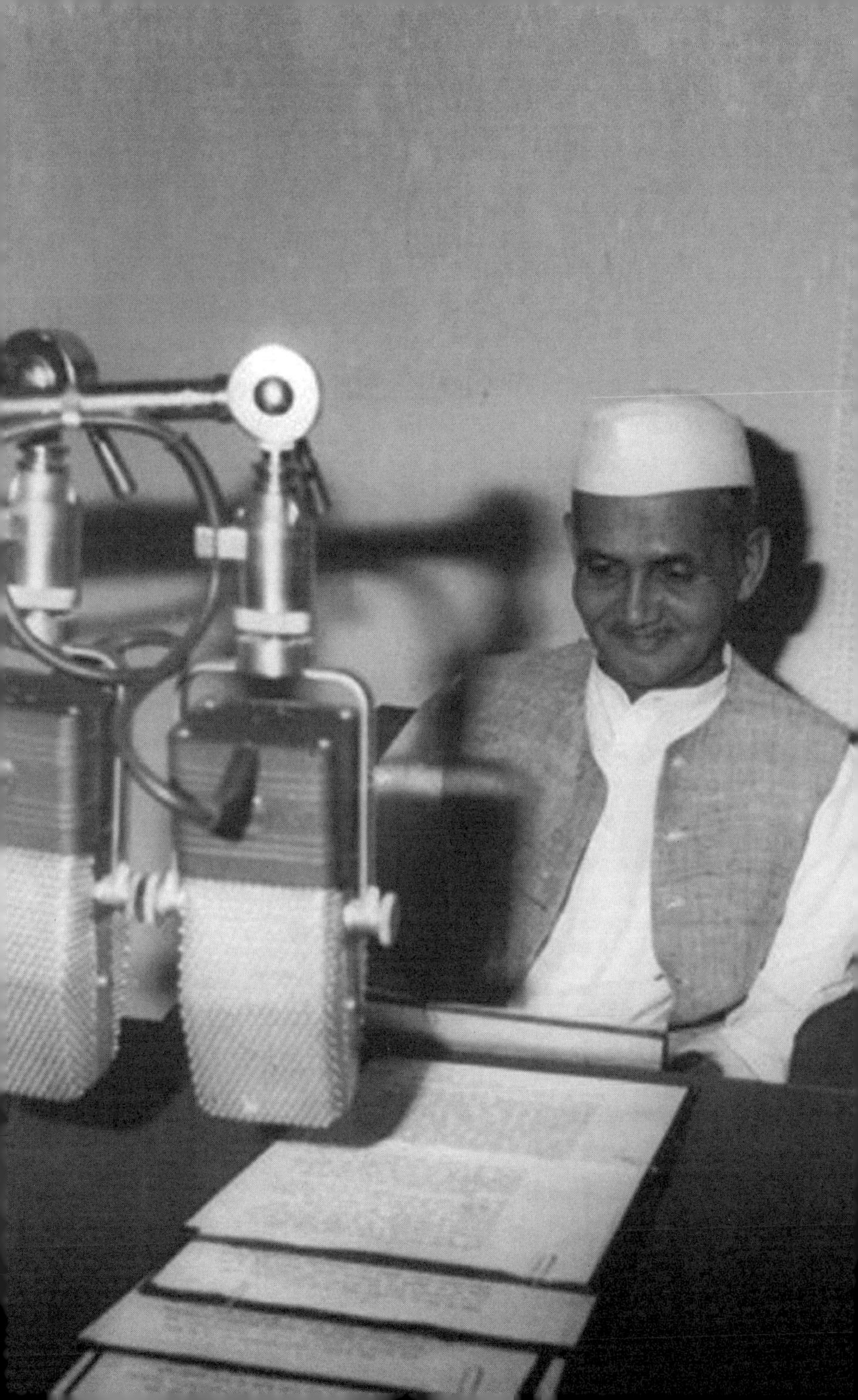

Babuji exemplified this saying and he passed on that wisdom to me. My roots were the same as his.

From my childhood, I had dreamt of becoming a doctor and serving people especially in the rural areas. I used to read elementary books on homeopathy and started distributing medicines on the basis of this acquired knowledge. I was just a boy, but sitting in the lawn and handing those pills to the best of my understanding, I became 'doctor saheb'. But with Babuji's sudden death, this dream got shattered. It was extremely painful to lose Babuji, and it was equally searing to accept the collapse of my dreams. Both were irreparable but terrible losses.

Believe me, with Babuji's demise, the entire family returned to an ordinary Indian household. There was nothing that existed for Babuji except the nation. He never did anything for himself or for the family. When he was alive, I had a theoretical understanding of poverty, but with his death I experienced its reality. This is a bitter truth of life.

I had scaled heights since then and my stay in Shakti Bhavan only reinforced my understanding of life at its

▲ The disciple and the mentor

high point vis-à-vis life at the grass roots that I saw from the windows of this tall building. During my tenure as minister there had been many heart wrenching incidents and many scenes that tugged at my heart frequently giving me nightmarish vision of poverty so visible on the streets. My mind used to swirl with dreams of my going in an official car with applause from an admiring crowd only to be jolted out by the sight of a small child on a heap of sand. The contrast between my satiated life as a minister and the hungry child on the road was too painful for me. Almost like Siddharth (Gautam Buddha of his early days), I needed to share my agony with my companions, but there was none who could understand me. How I wish I could don a stethoscope and go to my simple rural folks and provide them relief from pain and sickness. But reality bites in every sense of the term. The truth was that I was not a doctor, but a minister in public service sitting in Shakti Bhavan, far from the people who needed me.

It was in times like these that I received support and comfort from Meera. She had once asked me to honour the commitment I had given to my friend that I would visit him and his family for dinner. I had gone there reluctantly, but the visit gave me the wisdom not to be cynical or scornful of friends, who are genuine with no self-interest.

Babuji was an eternal source of strength at times of crisis. My decision to renounce positions of power was often misinterpreted by one and all as acts of cowardice. I wish my critics had taken the trouble to understand my depth of feelings instead of belittling my emotions. I have great regard for Gandhiji though I had not met him. I have always made the effort to understand his views on sacrifice, non-violence, religion and tolerance. It is difficult to understand Gandhiji if one does not live those principles he had stood for. If Babuji had been alive, I would have asked him about Gandhiji's religion in today's conflicting world. Babuji would have given me the insight into the act of renunciation that was at the core of all Gandhian philosophy. Without him, I faced this huge dilemma; to be or not to be a Minister; to be or not to be a committed server of the poor and the needy. The questions 'when' and 'how' to take the big step of relinquishing my charge as Minister and returning to my roots to serve the people disturbed my equanimity. I recalled Babuji's dilemma when he became Prime Minister. He made a visit to his village in Allahabad constituency and was shocked to see its backwardness, its lack of water supply which forced the villagers buy water. He was distressed and on returning home he told Amma: "The day I retire from politics, I will be here in this place to serve the people. Babuji couldn't return as he had desired. It was left to Amma to fulfill his dream. Nearly ten months after Babuji's demise, she came to the village and founded a centre: 'Lal Bahadur Shastri Seva Niketan', the main aim of which was to serve the people there, raise their standard of living and bring about a change to make them self-reliant.

At that time, I could not lend adequate assistance to Amma at the foundation. I had taken up a bank job to provide financial assistance to the family. Bank work absorbed all my time and I was restless, torn between serving the bank and serving the people. Bank service was limited and my desire was for a bigger arena where I could reach out to a large number of people. Whenever anyone needed help from within the family or outside, I was willing to lend them assistance that I could possibly muster. I continued to work almost like a politician and I decided to enter active politics so that I had greater opportunity to serve my people. Indiraji understood my passion and encouraged me in my decision to give up a salaried job to enter politics.

Before long I realized that to be a politician, one has to develop thick skin. There were a number of occasions when I used to go to meet senior politicians. Some of them were gracious to meet me; there were others who refused to recognize me. But these things did not deter me from pursuing my passion for active politics though I waited long, till 1980 to get a foothold in the political arena. But the process of meeting politicians of all hues and working with selfless dedication as an ordinary party worker toughened me and matured me as a politician.

I was brought up in a political atmosphere. Though I was young and was dreaming of a medical profession, I was curious to see and learn how Babuji managed his political career with its knotty political issues. There were instances when Babuji's approach and behaviour were beyond the comprehension of a fifteen-year old. I used to get irritated and frustrated, for a teenager's immature views on life were different from an older person's mature and experienced reflections. Whenever there was conflict of opinions between Babuji and me, I used to question him. Babuji's answer, with its idealism and pragmatism would open my eyes to a newer perspective, what a young mind could not envision. He let me see a new world, a new expanse.

Babuji as Prime Minister had in his daily schedule given time for meeting people in the mornings. Many came to meet him, greet him and seek his assistance if they had personal problems. I used to be with him during these morning meetings when I came to learn about people from different walks of life, each one of them speaking about his individual as well as collective problems. Babuji never denied me this opportunity; on the contrary, he encouraged me to develop both an interest in people and the ability to empathize with their difficulties. For me it was a learning experience and especially so when Babuji explained to me the solutions he offered to redress their grievances.

It was a very special day for me when I got time to take a stroll with him on our lawns. He was talking to me while we were walking, sometimes serious, sometimes laughing and in a relaxed mood. In between people came and went after narrating their stories seeking Babuji's guidance. While this was happening, I noticed a German lady taking pictures of Babuji and me. She had been given prior permission to capture Babuji in his different moods. As a young boy, I got excited at the prospect of being photographed with Babuji and tried to look graceful and impressive. It is a pity that I did not note the address of the German lady. As a result I had no access to those special photographs.

That was the day when the then Home Minister Shri.Gulzari Lal Nanda came to the house with an industrialist. When Babuji was informed, he looked at his watch and said that he had still some more time to meet the general public and that he would meet them soon after. He asked his personal secretary to make them comfortable in the sitting room of his office. But within minutes the two of them had left. I was a bit upset and wondered if there was an element of discourtesy in Babuji's request to them to wait till his meeting with the public was over. Babuji still had five minutes for the public and he told me that he would talk to me later. I felt depressed and waited for him. After five minutes Babuji came to me and asked me if I was annoyed. He took me to one side of the lawn and pointed to a tree. I saw an old man. Pointing him, Babuji asked me if I knew him. I said: "No. I don't know him." Babuji said; "He comes from a poor family from a far off hilly region. It is difficult to say how long he and his family had stayed hungry. He has spent the little savings he had made to make this trip to Delhi to meet the Prime Minister and apprise him of his impoverished condition. Babuji then pointed to another tree where a woman stood, waiting to meet him. Babuji told me that she had come from a far off village in South India with the money she collected after mortgaging her jewellery. She also had a problem to narrate to her leader. Babuji continued: "Sunil, tell me, should I have left these people and not heard them for the sake of meeting my Home Minister who has easy access to me all through the day. The Industrialist who accompanied him is capable of making 20 visits, flying from Bombay to Delhi to meet the Prime Minister. But do you think these people who have come from so far can make another trip to meet me if I had given them no time." I realized how small I was in the presence of Babuji's greatness. This small man had a big heart. In his gentle way, he had given me a lesson to see the difference between the wealthy and influential members of the society and the poor unnoticed people who trudge through difficult ways to be at the Prime Minister's door. Both had the same purpose—the attention of the Prime Minister and his intervention to solve their problems—but Babuji knew who needed him more and hence his priority to listen to the more deprived group than the influential one. Babuji had a unique way of teaching. I made a promise to myself that like Babuji, I will pay greater attention to the needs of the poor and do my utmost to assist them. When I recall all these precious moments with Babuji when he gave me the penetrating insight into the life and condition of a majority of poor people in our country, I wonder if Babuji had the foresight to see that I was not cut out to be a medical doctor, but had the sensitivity, empathy and potential to serve the common man as he did.

Yet another memorable instance comes to my mind. This was during the Indo-Pakistan war in 1965, when Babuji was a year into the Prime Minister's office. Early in the morning, Babuji woke me up and asked me to accompany him. I was excited—an outing with Babuji was

देशकी रक्षाके लिए हम खून बहा देंगे

प्रधानमंत्री श्री शास्त्री की चेतावनी

(हमारे नगर संवाददाता द्वारा)

हमारी सेना पाक घुस-पैठके अड्डों तक जाएगी

शास्त्री द्वारा पाकिस्तानी चाल विफल करनेके निश्चयकी घोषणा

(हमारे विशेष प्रतिनिधि द्वारा)

रूस का कश्मीर के मामले में मध्यस्थता का प्रस्ताव ?

Force will be met with force, Shastri warns Pakistan

By Our Political Correspondent

NEW DELHI, Aug 13—The Prime Minister today warned Pakistan that force would be met with force and aggression against India would never be allowed to succeed.

Broadcasting to the Nation tonight, Mr Shastri said that Pakistani infiltrations into Kashmir, coming as it did after its naked aggression along the Kutch border last April, necessitated a re-examination of Indo-Pakistani relations as a whole.

Mr Shastri declared: Pakistan has probably taken a deliberate decision to keep up an atmosphere of tension. We have, therefore, to reckon with the situation in a realistic manner."

"India," the Prime Minister said, "had to reorientate its thinking ... its policies to deal ...

... loyalty of the motherland in the severest trial it is facing today.

He reminded the people that across India's borders were ... forces which threatened the continuance of India as a free and independent country.

The Prime Minister said that the Government would allow no ... who indulged in ...

पाकिस्तान लड़ाई का रास्ता छोड़े : शास्त्रीजी

ताशकंद-वार्ता में शांति के लिए भरसक प्रयत्न का आश्वासन

(हमारे कार्यालय संवाददाता द्वारा)

नई दिल्ली, १ जनवरी।

पाक के बल-प्रयोग का प्रतिरोध होगा : शास्त्री

मामूली सीमा-विवाद वार्ता से हल किए जाएं

very special to me at all times. I asked him if I should pack my bags to which he replied there was no need. It was still dark when we got into the car with his most trustworthy driver, Rajaram at the wheel.

We were driving towards Palam and with excitement I asked: "Are we going to the airport? Why did you tell me not to pack my bags?" Babuji with his finger on his lips hinted to me to keep quiet. At the airport we were welcomed by Lt. Generals and Major-Generals and they took us to an Indian Air Force plane. It was called 'Pushpak'. After we were seated, Babuji told me that he was taking me on an outing to Pakistan.

I was on cloud nine, literally and metaphorically speaking. I was flying high up in the skies, sitting next to Babuji, the Prime Minister of India. I had been close to Babuji in the past but this closeness was very special. We landed at the air base of Halwara which had been attacked by Pakistan. But thanks to the prompt counter response of Indian soldiers, the attack was foiled. We could see the marks of the enemy shells in the nearby buildings, but the airbase could not be stormed.

From Halwara we were escorted to Burki where the national tricolour was flying. I bowed in respect and prayed for the souls of those soldiers who had laid down their lives to keep the tricolour atop and fluttering in the skies. We were standing close to a military tank and were informed

▲ Getting ready to defend the nation

that many of the military tanks had been deployed to keep a watch over Lahore radio station and open rapid fire to repulse any attack from the enemy side.

I was fifteen-years old. I was always keen to know and understand the people of Pakistan, their culture, their ways of living, their tradition and customs. But what I saw before me was sheer devastation. All houses had been destroyed. So were the Patton tanks, broken and abandoned under the shell impact of the Indian army. While I was lost in thought and trying to come to terms with life and destruction in times of war, the officers of the Indian army requested Babuji to stand on one of the tanks and be photographed. I cherish those moments—moments of pride at the success of the Indian army as well as moments of deep sadness at the death and devastation that war threw up. Whenever I see those photographs of Babuji standing on a tank, I re-live those moments and experience those feelings once again.

As a young boy, I also wanted to stand on the tank. The Major was warm and made me stand up as I had wished. Though everyone present was against it, Babuji wanted to visit the Ichukki canal. This was a strategic place with one side of the canal monitored by Indian soldiers and facing them on the other side were their Pakistani counterparts. The army officials were afraid of the Prime Minister's safety and persuaded him not to go there. But Babuji said:

> **"Not one but several soldiers had laid down their lives here. Then, at this moment, should I think just about my life? I want to encourage them. I have come here to appreciate them."**

These words still echo in my ears. He was not a soldier; he had never wielded a gun nor would he ever. But he was no coward. He had the moral strength of a leader who could be one of them, who could show that he is a soldier in mind and heart even without the formal training given to a professional soldier. His "Jai Jawan" was his great salute to the defenders of the nation. The Generals and the officers made 4–6 rings around him as Babuji slowly made his way towards the Ichukki canal. No harm could and should come to the nation's small man with a big mind and heart. Babuji addressed the soldiers, applauded their bravery and appreciated their loyalty. While he was engaged in talking to them, I almost mulishly told the officers that I would not leave the place unless I touched the water in the canal.

Though I was refused, I insisted that I should be taken close to the water. Finally one of the Majors yielded to my stubborn request and took me near the canal. Hardly had I touched the water, there were a host of Pakistani soldiers up and ready to shoot me down. The Major held me firmly and ran swifter than air and brought me back safe. A nightmarish and disastrous incident was averted by the Major's presence of mind. Even today I get jitters when I recall this incident that would have been tragic.

On our return to Delhi, we visited the hospitals where the injured soldiers were being treated. I was of an impressionistic age when the sight of wounded soldiers was likely to inflame my passion and develop total hatred for the Pakistanis. Babuji was a very wise man. Without letting my anger turn to vengeful ire he told me: "Sunil, our soldiers safeguard our country. This war is between two countries and not between two people. That is why I have told our soldiers that as far as possible the common people should not become victims of the war." Babuji was full of humanity and kindness. He spoke from his heart with honestly. He was a politician with a difference—the language he used was not a political language. Unlike the general rung of politicians, he packaged politics into humanity and not humanity into politics.

Babuji went and sat on the cots where the soldiers were lying. He held their hands, talked to them, comforted them and blessed them with his hands on their heads. One of the soldiers was Major Bhupinder Singh who had taken the entire shelling on his body. As Babuji took his hands with warmth and love, the brave soldier's eyes were brimming with tears. Babuji asked him why being a

> "Sunil, our soldiers safeguard our country. This war is between two countries and not between two people. That is why I have told our soldiers that as far as possible the common people should not become victims of the war."

renowned Major in the Indian army should he have tears. The Major replied in words that are too difficult to re-tell. He said: "Sir, I am a Major in the Indian army—the army which is counted among the topmost in the world. I don't have tears in my eyes because my death is near or that I may live for a few more days, but that despite being a Major, I am not being able to stand up and salute my Prime Minister." Babuji's eyes also filled with tears—the first time I had seen tears in his eyes. He had always shown himself to be man of extraordinary mental and emotional strength, but in the face of such fierce loyalty and patriotism, even Babuji could not control his emotions. I could not bear to see Babuji's tears and I moved out and got into the car. A few minutes later, Babuji came to me and asked me: "Why did you go away?" I could not reply as I was choking with emotions. Babuji did not probe further as he understood my state of mind. He saw the fan in the car and switched it off while he asked me who had switched it on. "I did", I replied. Babuji said: "Didn't you see the soldiers here don't have fans. They are lying here in great discomfort and still you had the thought of using a fan for yourself."

I did not look him in the eye. I was aware of his looks that revealed his high expectations from me; he wanted me to be somewhat similar to him in nature—selfless, altruistic, patriotic and above all a people's person. He had his way of talking through his eyes.

Amma had been with me for two Holis though she preferred staying in Delhi during festivals. Her presence had always been of comfort to me. She relieved me of my loneliness and made the absence of Babuji less haunting. It was unusually hot in Lucknow during this period where Holi marked the departure of winter and the onset of spring. I did not switch on the fan, somewhere deep down I remembered our visit to Major Bhupinder Singh. My wife was surprised to see me not using a fan. She switched it on and I switched it off. Meera was not able to understand my action but somehow I did not feel like unburdening the deep pain within me. This is true of every individual. Even the closest person cannot experience one's pain—both physical and mental. one may feel sad and disturbed, but understanding and experiencing another person's agony in full measure is not given to anyone of us. Switching on and off the fan brought back memories of my visit to the army hospital with Babuji way back in 1965, and Babuji's way of empathizing with their condition by personally experiencing their hard and uncomfortable living conditions.

As energy minister of Uttar Pradesh, my office was Sachivalaya Annexe where I had earlier lived with Babuji when he was the state's Police (Home) Minister. The location of my office was the verandah of our house where we used to play as kids. I was just a year old then. Amma told me that Babuji used to be late coming home from his office. One day after waiting for him till late in the evening, he came and I took him to the top floor verandah and pointed to him the sentry at the gate. Babuji and Amma understood my innocent childish gesture that meant getting Babuji arrested by the sentry if he came late again. Babuji must have made a casual mention of this incident to his colleagues, but it somehow reached the newspaper reporters who splashed the headline: "Son threatens Police Minister to be arrested by the police." I recalled this while sitting at home in Lucknow. Human mind is as sharp as a computer. It can take us back and forth in time and that too, without a mouse click. The memories of my stay with Babuji and the press coverage of my innocent remark came surging in my mind and I chuckled to myself. Meera who was in and out of the room saw me smiling all by myself and asked me: " What are you doing here sitting alone and laughing?" Again I stayed silent as those childhood

▲ Oath ceremony to fulfill Shastriji's legacy

memories are mine and cannot be experienced by others who had not witnessed those times.

During Holi, we had plenty of home made sweet. On one such occasion, Vibhor (my youngest son) came with a Gujiya in his mouth and another in his hand which he thrust into my mouth. I am fond of Gujiya. Amma's Gujiyas were special and despite her failing health she had made them and other delicacies for the festival. My son made a classic statement that he had decided to eat nothing but Gujiya from then onwards. He hugged me and told

▲ Holi: Festival without barriers

me to request Dadi to visit us during Holi without fail. His innocence and childishness reminded me of my early days. I had lovely memories of celebrating Holi with Babuji.

Those were the times when a lot of dignitaries including Ministers visited us and partook of all the delicacies that were prepared at home a week prior to the festival.

Though not fond of Holi, I loved playing with dry powder. Among the many who used to visit us, were a few labourers. They felt constrained to apply colour on our faces. Instead, they bent down and sought our blessings. But with all my childish enthusiasm, I coloured their faces and asked them to do so in return without shyness or inferiority. Babuji's sense of belonging to them, his rootedness with common people had made a great impact on my tender mind which has continued with me through my life. The labourers were delighted to be invited to share Holi celebrations with us. I was excited and happy to be hugged and greeted by everybody, big or small. Our house used to be full of people and the lawns where we met them were a riot of colours. During one such occasion, Babuji called me in and asked me to find out who was at the gate and bring him in. He was Kanchhi's father, one who used to clean our home. He had his fists closed and he bent down at Babuji's feet to open his fists that contained red colour. He had such respect for Babuji that he wanted to put the colour at his feet and not smear it on his face. Babuji held him back, saying "Today is the day to hug and colour is to be smeared on face and not on the feet." He smeared colour on Kanchhi's, father and invited him to colour his face. Babuji later said that Holi was one festival that brought him so close to his people that given the option, he would celebrate it throughout the year. Holi, he said, is a festival of equality that erased all differences imposed on the society by an outdated caste system. It is one day in the year when both the high and the low join together in a spirit of fun and bonhomie. No other festival can bridge class distinctions and cultivate humanity but Holi.

Babuji's words were always truthful. Before I filed my nomination in Gorakhpur, I went to Babuji's Samadhi and took an oath that I would do my utmost to bring to reality a small part of Babuji's dream for a classless and casteless society where all people will live as Indians. My decision to enter politics was my own and I had no time to discuss it with Meera in detail. We had a good understanding and I knew that whatever I decided would have Meera's assent. Nevertheless when I left Delhi to begin a new life as a full fledged politician, I asked Meera whether she liked this decision of mine to take up new challenges that were often daunting especially to the one who was making his first foray into the world of politics. Meera remained quiet and I repeated my question. Had she remained silent I would have lectured her about what urged me to join politics and what my priorities would be as an active politician. I had got into the habit of talking continuously if I had a listening audience. Meera simply took her hand and placed it on my lips and said: "whichever path you choose, I' will be with you. But I would definitely like to add—I have never seen Babuji. He had died much before we got married. Whatever I have heard about him from you and from other family members, keeping all that in mind, I would like you always to try and not do anything that would raise a question on his integrity." I was astounded at her incisive observation, her respect for Babuji whom she had not met, and her remarkable faith in his integrity. She did not ask anything for herself; she only wanted Babuji's reputation honoured and preserved. Deep within I knew that today's politics is not the same as it was in Babuji's times. The changed political atmosphere has made it difficult to be good and honest. Still I promised her and spoke to her about the oath I had taken at Babuji's Samadhi. Till then I had not shared my personal feelings with anyone. But I opened up before Meera and told her that I had pledged that I shall never do anything that would dishonour and defame Babuji even if I failed to do anything to bring credit to his name. Though I could not find words to adequately describe my thoughts, I was able to assure Meera that I will prove worthy of being my father's son.

Meera said that she understood me well but that she still wanted to know what I had planned before beginning a new life as a politician. I had full faith in Meera that she would go all the distance with me in whatever I did. We were bonded to each other and sharing and living together was a matter of faith for both of us. Meera came from a salaried class. Her father had fixed hours at work and so did I when I was working in the bank. But a politician has no control on time. There were many evenings when I could not return home and kept her waiting. This was the price she had to pay as a politician's wife. But Meera had anticipated this change and was prepared for it. Little did I know that she had an idea of what it would be to wait and how difficult it would be if I was held up. For the first time she told to me about her desire to meet Babuji when she was very young. She had heard that Babuji was expected in

Jaipur where she was living then. She desperately wanted to see him and decided to go alone to a place that Babuji was to pass during his visit. She couldn't say why she felt that Babuji was her own and that she had a right to see him. Babuji passed in front of her. She waved to him with great enthusiasm. The small big man waved back and she felt that he was specially responding to her. All this had happened when she was young. Though she had not been with him, she always felt his presence in the house where she lived as a daughter-in-law. Babuji's fleeting visit had given her the insight into the busy schedule of a politician. Hence her narration of her childhood image of Babuji confirmed that she was with me in my new vocation and was ready for the changes that would ensue in her family life.

We had been married for seven years. She had never once spoken about Babuji in this period. But she felt it necessary to tell me about her respect and reverence for Babuji to assure me that she would be with me in all my efforts to emulate him.

After the elections, we started a new innings. The only thing that bothered her was my long absence from home sometimes extending to 4–5 days. She requested me to return home in the evenings. But such a routine was not possible for me. Many times I had desperately tried to reach home, but couldn't do so. I then remembered how I used to be angry with Babuji when I was a child and needed him all the time. I often complained to him that we were denied his love and affection. The same thing was repeated in my family. Whenever I came late and saw my children sleeping, I wondered if they also thought the same. Would they also wonder what kind of a father I was and whether I had fatherly responsibilities at all. But Babuji never got annoyed or shouted at us when we complained. Unlike him, I am irritable, short-tempered and excitable. I don't have his patience, his calm demeanour. But I have his example in front of me that gives me the awareness of my weakness and the resolve to rise above it. When I got the ticket to contest the elections, I had to resign from the bank. I had to put up with many unpleasant situations prior to relinquishing my position. I was able to face them without losing patience, thanks to the example Babuji had set before me.

The bank job had given me experiences that helped me to grow into a responsible man. I wrote a short letter of resignation and handed it to the bank's authority. The person got up from his chair and came near me and blessed me. I had been a small time employee and he had been my officer. Things changed fast with the perception that I was on my way to becoming an important man. He had high regard for Babuji and asked me

लाल बहादुर शास्त्री

मरणोपरान्त

मैं भारत का राष्ट्रपति, सर्वपल्लि राधाकृष्णन, व्यक्तिगत गुणों के लिए आपके सम्मानार्थ, भारत रत्न प्रदान करता हूं।

स० राधाकृष्णन

राष्ट्रपति

नई दिल्ली

दिनांक 20 अप्रैल 1966
30 चैत्र 1888

▲ Etched for posterity

to complete the tasks Babuji had left incomplete with his sudden demise.

There were many reactions to my action—of stepping out from the bank and entering politics. Some were happy and proud that I was on my way to scale great heights. Some were sad that we were parting ways and I was not going to be with them any longer. I also knew that there were quite a few who would be critical of my step and would have made nasty comments to the effect that I had been a failure in the bank and hence was opting for politics. They almost predicted failure in my new task as well. Some of these criticisms annoyed me. But that was not the time to retaliate. I understood the need for tolerance and I resolved to prove my critics wrong. I decided to put in more than one hundred percent of my effort to achieve success in what I had decided to do.

One of my close friends to whom I had shown my letter of resignation cautioned me about giving up a secure job in search of a foothold in politics which would pull me down like quick sand. He said that I was young and had a family to look after.

We went out and discussed it over a small snack of chaat from a hawker. After a lengthy discussion, he also came round to my view point. This was in 1980. Three years ealier, I had approached Mrs. Indira Gandhi and her son, Sanjay Gandhi to give me a Lok Sabha ticket. Indiraji advised me to meet the then Congress President, Mr. Dev Kant Barua. He told me to contest from Allahabad, which was Babuji's constituency and which had later in 1967 been that of my elder brother, Hari Bhaiya. He said that he would provide for cars and all publicity material and that I should file my nomination.

I was just 27 years old when I got the ticket for 1977. I had been working as per the directions of Indiraji, but this was a bonus from her to me. My hardwork of those years had paid a handsome dividend. I returned home after meeting Indiraji—happy and excited. Amma told me that I was a little hasty in joining politics. I had a ready answer; "If not today, then tomorrow. After all we have to complete Babuji's unfinished tasks. Where does the question of early or late arise in this? Let us not leave for tomorrow what we can do today…".

I flew to Lucknow only to be called back to Delhi. Indiraji met me in her office and said that the party had decided to field older and experienced people instead of new and younger people. It did not take me long to understand. Babu Jagjivan Ram and Hemvati Nandan Bahaguna had resigned and Indiraji thought it best to give the older people the tickets. I was shattered. I could not control my tears which were not lost on Indiraji's perspicuous eyes.

I had to return to my bank work. The workload in the bank took over everything.

Babuji used to call me *Bambaddas*. It was because I was not the one to taste success and fail. My destiny was such that I never reached the heights I dreamt and therefore the return to ordinary mundane work was never a great disappointment. I have always been an emotional person, something that I had inherited from Babuji. I had a dream of becoming a doctor that was intertwined with social service to alleviate the physical pain and suffering of the poor and the penniless people. Then I fancied climbing the political ladder and finally landed back in the bank job. True to *Bambaddas*, as Babuji called me, I accepted what destiny had mapped out for me. My passion for service to the people had been kindled by Babuji. He had advised me when I was still in my teens that I should serve people not only through the channel of politics, but whenever and wherever opportunity arose, I should seize it and serve the poor and the needy. That was when I told him of my dream of serving people after doing medicine. I was far too young to understand what the profession of a doctor was like and how it differed from politics. I just had this intense feeling that I should be of some use to the people of our nation. Sharing their pain and caring for them became a burning desire within me.

As a child, I had read about Siddharth (Gautam Buddha), though I can't say for sure that he was my role model. But in my later years, I felt that Siddharth's influence had left an indelible impact on me that made me take up social service as my vocation. It is strange that I thought of the poor people at a time when we lived reasonably well and poverty and lack of money were far removed from our world of reality. I had not seen Amma's struggle to run the family and feed my elder brother and sisters when Babuji was in jail. I was born much later when financial strains were more like tales from the past. From time to time Babuji had spoken to me of those difficult days to make me aware of reality. Thus my dream of becoming a doctor was buttressed by my passion for reaching out to the poor in the villages. I was drawn towards the villages and the poor people and I dreamt of opening a dispensary for them. I told Babuji that later I wanted to open a nursing home for those living in backward areas that had no medical facilities to offer. Babuji was not only receptive to my idea, he was happy and proud that his son fully shared his own

▲ Amma paying homage at Vijay Ghat

concern for the poor people in the villages. But today when I recall his shining eyes, I discern strange feelings of hidden misgivings behind them. I now wonder whether Babuji knew that all my dreams were just flights of fancy, far removed from reality. Everytime I talked to him about becoming a doctor, he had a strange look of bafflement and concern that my dreams may crash in the world of harsh reality.

With his death, my dreams and fancies also died. At the tender age of 16, I became an adult. I was aware of my responsibility and I did not allow my dreams to come in the way of what I had to do at that point of time. I accepted a job in a bank—not with the excitement of a young man getting his first job while still a teenager, but with a terrifying sadness at the collapse of my dreams. I cried deep within myself at the unpredictable vagaries of fortune.

I remember Amma taking me inside Babuji's room where his footwear and his ashes were kept. For me it was like Sri Ram's padukas as I stood before them in obeisance to a great soul that had sparked the right values of kindness, compassion and selfless service within me. I could not stop crying as I was haunted by the inexplicable role destiny had played in my life. Amma was a great comforter. A woman of great wisdom, she said if service was my motto, I should accept any form of work and find ways to serve the people. She said that it was an opportunity for me to learn from life's experiences that were sad, harsh and disappointing.

Her words raised my spirits. I could recall the song of the famous group ABBA:

I have a dream, a song to sing
To help me cope with anything
If you see the wonder of a fairy tale
You can take the future even if you fail
I believe in angels
Something good in everything I see
I believe in angels
When I know the time is right for me
I'll cross the stream—I have a dream

I have a dream, a fantasy
To help me through reality
And my destination makes it worth the while
Pushing through the darkness still another mile
I believe in angels
Something good in everything I see
I believe in angels
When I know the time is right for me
I'll cross the stream—I have a dream
I'll cross the stream—I have a dream

I understood my dream: to serve the masses and I knew my angels: my Babuji and Amma And I learnt to see something good in everything even in my return to my bank job without becoming a politician.

On my first day at the bank, I was greeted with warmth and love because I was the son of a worthy Prime Minister. My seniors and colleagues had great respect for Babuji who in his short tenure as Prime Minister had shown the nation a new path of discovering itself. The slogan 'Jai Jawan, Jai Kisan' was not an empty slogan. It galvanized people to action to redeem the glory and dignity of the nation. I experienced the burden of that love and respect I received from people from all walks of life. I realized that I was Babuji's son and I had to shoulder the huge responsibility of living true to his honour and ideals. I was in a sense no longer a free man to do what I wanted to do. Every action of mine would be under scrutiny as I was my father's son.

During the initial days of training, people were keen to know about Babuji and his simple life style. I was not getting irritated at being asked the same questions again and again; on the contrary, everytime I spoke about Babuji, I understood him better. His words and action gave me a deeper understanding of the little great man. I was good at my work, blessed with quick uptake of all the duties assigned to me. While it took four days for others to understand what they were told, it took me just four hours. That is why all through my life I had never suffered from lack of time. I did my work in good time and had enough time on hand to attend to other people's needs.

Soon I realized that my working area was limited. I needed to work on a higher and larger level. I wanted to break free of this pedestrian routine. But there are no shortcuts in life. I was still young and was not considered mature to take up greater responsibilities. In the year 1969 while I was serving the bank, Mrs. Indira Gandhi who had succeeded Babuji's as Prime Minister announced the nationalization of banks in the country. Banks that were the property of a few people now were opened to benefit society on a large scale. A reporter came to me and asked me about my views on bank nationalization. My bank was also one amongst the many banks that had been nationalized. There were criticisms and skepticism about the correctness of this decision. No one had any idea of how the benefits will trickle to the people. Personally I had not thought deeply of its benefit or loss. Still I answered: "That amount which till now was available only to a few people will now be accessible to the masses. The dream that our Prime Minister has will definitely prove successful. This is my firm belief."

In 1971, I was promoted as the Branch Manager of a small village branch Kakori, in Uttar Pradesh. I had to leave Delhi where I was an accountant. I accepted the transfer and the new appointment without thinking about what future prospects it held for me. Certainly I felt the pain of moving out of Delhi, away from all my near and dear ones. I was once more taken to village life.

It was no longer fanciful as I had imagined in my early years. I was face to face with poverty and backwardness and I understood the meaning of deprivation. To begin with, I developed an escapist attitude by going to Lucknow as and when an opportunity came my way. Lucknow was about 15 kms away from Kakori. One day I missed the train to Lucknow and started strolling around the village. I stood in the midst of the fields and felt a sense of closeness to nature. It did not look alien to me and I discovered a new sense of fellowship with the village and its surroundings. I remembered my last visit to the backward area in Bhopal prior to Babuji's fatal visit to Tashkent. That village in Bhopal was even more backward than Kakori. It struck me that all those promises I had made to the villagers in Bhopal had come to nothing. This posting in Kakori appeared to me as a punishment posting for my failure to fulfill those promises. I recalled in a flash that Babuji used to talk about Kakori as the place that had witnessed the big train robbery when the English treasury had been looted. A new horizon opened before me. I did not feel distant from the poor villagers. I felt as though I had known them for ages and they were my own people.

Instead of returning home, I went to meet the head of the village, Kamil Khan. Kamil Khan took me to Mohammad Sabir Saheb. They were surprised why I was interested to have a re-look at old records which no one had touched for so many years. Initially he was reluctant to take me to the place where the great train robbery had taken place. But since I was insistent and determined, he took me near the Railway track and showed me the place where the English treasury had been looted by the freedom fighters. There was a heap of mud kept as a symbol of the Freedom fighters' bold action against the mighty British. He was astonished that after so many years I had wanted to see this place. I stood before the heap in reverence. History unfolded in front of me and for the moment, I became a part of that glorious chapter of our history. A historical moment had been reduced just to a mud heap!

I resolved to create a proper monument of that mud heap for posterity to remember and pay homage to our freedom fighters. The next day when I opened the bank register, the names of the village people brought before my eyes yesterday's people who had taken part in that train robbery. The rural area of Kakori took on a new meaning for me. The feeling of belonging to the village, the sense of rootedness and fraternal closeness took possession of me. Kakori posting was indeed a gift to me. I could translate into concrete action Babuji's slogan "Jai Jawan, Jai Kisan". As Manager of the Bank, as the son of the great man who brought new respect to the farmers, I seized the opportunity to give loans for seeds, for the oxen and for pump sets and other farming expenditure. The villagers are simple folks who are scared of documents and paper formalities associated with taking loans. They hesitate to come to the bank. Well, as the saying goes, if Mohammad cannot go to the mountain, then the mountain comes to Mohammad. Of course travel through a village is not easy. There are no motorable roads. At best one can use a bicycle as an alternative to walking. But even cycling separates the rider from the villagers. To be a part of them, one necessarily had to walk like them.

The village people are guarded and do not open up easily. One can never gauge the truth behind their actions and words. They have their own way of living and are particular to live with dignity. To seek help or redressal from an outsider is not for them. I had the task

▲ My inspiration and mentor

of helping out one Ramavadh who had mortgaged his land and bulls and was in need of redeeming them from the moneylender. This was precisely the bank's mandate and I was thankful to the bank for giving me this opportunity to serve the poor villagers. I could carry forward the rich legacy of Babuji by assisting the villagers with bank loans and bank schemes. Whatever I learnt in Kakori had stood by me when I entered politics. I am grateful to God for providing me with such an opportunity to serve people at the grassroots level. Kakori became a part of my life and years later in 1983, I took Mrs. Indira Gandhi there to lay the foundation of the memorial at the village mud heap.

Babuji had inherited Nehru's mantle to steer the Nation to development and self-sufficiency, to reach great heights in science and technology and gain international recognition as a nation that stood for Gandhian values of truth, peace and non-violence, a nation that stood for pluralism and secularism as a tribute to humanity. Babuji and later Mrs. Indira Gandhi continued Nehruji's legacy to expand it further and today the nation is a transformed nation reaping the benefits of the solid foundation laid in those days. In my small way, I have been the inheritor of Babuji's legacy and I have not faulted in preserving that heritage. The advice he gave before leaving for Tashkent, to go to the rural areas in Madhya Pradesh and collect just about ₹ 10,000 helped me understand the majority of our people in remote areas and their hardships and sufferings. When I was in confusion with regard to resigning my bank job and contesting for elections, I had stood before Babuji's Samadhi and prayed and picked up the chit that directed me towards politics. Again it was Amma's direction that I should consult Babuji whenever I was in a dilemma to choose between two alternatives. Thanks to the great influence of my parents—Babuji and Amma, I had developed a keen empathy for the poor people of India. They have been my guiding force all through my life. They have been a silent influence on me to accept life's dispensations for good or bad. I had never taken a decision without going to Babuji's Samadhi and seeking his benedictions and direction.

This had happened when I filed my nominations from Gorakhpur. I was disappointed when Mrs. Gandhi decided to withdraw my candidature from Allahabad constituency in favour of older and more experienced politicians of her time. I was disappointed and I went and stood before Babuji's Samadhi. I was there for a long time as I needed his strength and courage to accept the collapse

◀ At Kakori with Indiraji

of my dream for a second time. I did not become a doctor; I could not become a politician. Destiny had denied the fruition of all my dreams. I raised my head and found a flower petal from the Samadhi Sthal on my forehead. Meera told me that the petal was Babuji's blessings on me to accept whatever life had in store for me. I kept the petal in my wallet and I returned to Lucknow. I was stronger and more resolute than ever to serve the masses in whatever capacity I was destined to hold. I was ready for any kind of sacrifice as long as every action of mine contributed to the betterment of my people. This is the lesson I had learnt from Babuji. I am the proud and humble inheritor of his legacy. My invaluable heritage is the idealism and nobility of my Babuji—Shri Lal Bahadur Shastri.

I pay respectful homage to my Babuji as I weave this humble tribute to him through this garland of words.

▼ Mentor and mother

Post Script

This is a revised edition of my earlier publication on my revered Babuji, Shri Lal Bahadur Shastri. To look at one's own work written nearly a quarter of a century back and to re-write it is an ambiguous privilege. A sense of satisfaction, an element of pride is there. But there is also a conflicting sense of embarrassment of what I now perceive to be the inadequacies in the earlier edition. Hence the impulse to re-write, to alter and amend has been irresistible and I have undertaken this task with a certainty that such a revision after a long passage of time will yield positive results.

Babuji, a day after signing the Tashkent Declaration that paved the way for a peaceful future co-existence between India and Pakistan died of a heart attack in 1966. He was the only Indian Prime Minister to have died in office while he was a state guest of a foreign government. He was a patriot—hero who after a successful war against Pakistan, spearheaded the move for peace between the two nations and just as the Nation was looking up to him as a Messiah of peace of a strong India, Shri Lal Bahadur Shastri suddenly passed away. The world paid tribute to this great man: "he came to power unexpectedly, and he left the world suddenly. Lal Bahadur Shastri was a star of great brightness in the history of India."

I dedicate this book to my parents who together had shaped me in their own image. I cannot think of Babuji without Amma. What I am today, I owe it to my parents who have instilled in me the Gandhian way of living—a life of simplicity, honesty and selfless service to the nation. Through this book, I want all my readers to understand the wholesome relationship that binds parents and their children.

I address this book especially to the millions of our young men and women who have no concept of the virtues of an elegant simple life that Gandhiji had practised and instilled in his followers.

Babuji, as I have addressed my father in this book lived a life that he advocated to his fellow Indians. He never preached, but he practised a life of a true human being that could be easily followed by all those who came in close contact with him. In all the different roles he had donned—son, husband, father, a selfless social worker, a committed and compassionate leader, a strong, firm and gentle Prime Minister, he showed himself to be an authentic human being. Amma was his perfect alter ego—humble in prosperity, noble in adversity, strong, self-effacing and empathetic to the suffering humanity. Like Babuji, Amma in all her varied roles as wife, mother, daughter-in-law and the first lady of the nation was strength and nobleness personified.

My purpose in re-writing this book is not to deify my father. I do not want my readers to look upon him as a holy cow but as one of the makers of a strong and self-sufficient India who has left behind a rich legacy of elegant simplicity that has been forgotten in the present century. The remarkable thing about Babuji was that he was a man of the masses who had a strong organic connection with the ordinary people of India. Unfortunately after the advent of LPG— Liberalization, Privatization and Globalization, our young educated elites in the urban areas have been reared on a pseudo concept of egalitarian capitalism that advocates self-interest, money, glamour and glitter. This has resulted in the widening of the chasm between the rich and the poor in our society. The only way to arrest the perceptible inegalitarianism is by understanding and appreciating the values of simple living that would spare sufficient resources to satisfy the needs of the many millions of our poor countrymen.

As a proud inheritor of my father's legacy I submit this book to my countrymen. Tolstoy said "the summation of millions of individuals' decisions and yearnings is the prime mover of history". I will be delighted and honoured if my book on Babuji's thoughts, values and ideals shapes the collective destiny of We, the people of India.

"...हम रहें या न रहें लेकिन यह झण्डा रहना चाहिए और देश रहना चाहिए। और मुझे विश्वास है कि यह झण्डा रहेगा, हम और आप रहें न रहें, लेकिन यह भारत का सिर उंचा होगा, भारत दुनिया के देशों में एक बड़ा देश होगा और शायद भारत दुनिया को कुछ दे भी सके। बहुत धन्यवाद। मैं आपसे निवेदन करूंगा कि तीन बार आप कृपा करके जयहिन्द बोलें।"

एक अनोखी यात्रा का अन्त

'Whether we live or not, this flag and this nation must live on. I have faith that this flag shall endure irrespective of our staying power and Bharat with her head high will be a Nation among nations, a powerhouse of new ideas for otheres to follow.
Thank You — Kindly repeat three times Jai Hind'

"Courage triumphs over adversity"